The Seven Epaulettes of Leadership

Work Love Love Work

Shawn Abrams

I0505721

© Copyright 2020 Shawn Abrams

abrams360media.com

All Rights Reserved.

No part of this publication may be reproduced, stored in a retrieval system, or transmitted, in any form or by any means, electronic, mechanical, photocopying, recording, or otherwise, without the written permission of the author.

Published in the United States of America

ISBN: 979-8615682810

abrams 360 media

We sometimes offer problems of the past to represent the reasons why. Well, we can also use those same problems to represent the response of, why not? Your why or why not will determine the experience you have.

Philotimo

I love this word, it has so many implications. It's interesting to me because it can be more easily assigned to experience rather than a black and white definition. The experience of leadership can change the world or just one life is *Philotimo*.

Leader's Creed

So many professionals have a creed. They could be considered words to live by for these people –Fireman, Police, and Military Personnel to name a few. Of note would be U.S. Army Paratroopers, as they have a long creed.

(This writer is somewhat biased as he has served as a paratrooper in the 82nd Airborne Division)

In fact, it's possible to jump out of an airplane and hit the ground quicker than you can recite the creed in its entirety. How's that for a challenge? Airborne!

Well, creeds include history, honor, readiness, service, strength, sacrifice, and the like. While the thought came to mind, I determined to create a creed for leaders. Now, I could have gone the route of a long or expansive narrative, but I resolved to use only two words.

They are: **I Will**

The people behind these words may not be acutely aware of the danger or discomfort that saying them may bring, but they decided. The decision itself was a displacement to the situation. Now, the intense fortitude they displayed will rally others to their side to assist or to shelter in place. Do you see that?

Two words can move a people and/or a situation.

Special thanks to

Galadriel Grace

Intro

Gentle Reminder: Leadership without the benefit of relationship is bullying, and a relationship without leadership is lost.

Leadership is a discipline for you, not the people you serve. Your reasonable service is to use it with faithful application to others, via mentoring and coaching in order to obtain the vision you hold.

Leadership is not about self, yourself, though it is about your vision. If to you, it's one and the same, you're wrong - people will see through this. They will feel like they're being used. If they did follow you at all, they will inevitably turn on you. A leader with no vision will only have their ego left, and because there is no vision, they will have to placate their ego. This will ultimately lead to an abuse of power. When this happened to nations, they called it a revolution.

To be clear, you either lead people to your vision or you lead them to your ego.

Today, it's a simple thing for computerized systems to capture time when an employee has clocked in or out. This level of accuracy is useful for payroll and ultimately our paychecks, but the same technology could be used to gauge employee wellness.

Why can't programmers add a short survey with just one question to answer after you punch-in? That one question could be answered with one of several options to describe their real-time disposition.

While this information may not be scientific, or 100% accurate, it is an indicator. This would allow senior leadership to know how those who respond are feeling. If they don't know and don't ask, how they be sure the people are work-ready? This is important for daily operations, but especially in the days leading up to a company-wide change.

Look at this, we may have more insight into the status of our vehicles than we do of our employees. There are approximately a hundred sensors in the average car today. They can tell us things like check the engine, low fuel, low tire pressure, etc. It's a diagnostic check of the various systems.

Let's be honest, despite some of the vehicle sensors going off we file the incident away into the back of our memory until a more convenient time to address the issue. So, receiving actionable reports is not enough, we must act on it in a reasonable timeframe.

This last statement speaks to the two umbrella topics I cover: *Leadership and Relationships.*

While writing this part of the book I paused to reflect here on what this means to me. I encourage you to do the same.

Why don't we have something similar in terms of diagnostic testing for our team? We depend on subordinate leaders to take care of these types of concerns, but if we don't have a leadership program in place, how sure are we that these leaders are aware of this? How sure are we that they can efficiently address the woes of the people?

This question is explored in greater detail as you read on. What about company culture? Is the company culture you describe on your website the same as the one that is prevalent in the different shops in your organization? If you're not sure if every employee feels like the company culture is a good one, and that they are a part of it, you're always going to lose staff, even if they don't leave the company. So, they're still working there – only, you're not truly leading them.

Let me use this analogy. Believing all is well because you're not asking for a status or because no unpleasant news has reached you, is troubling. This is the riptide effect. Do you know how easy it is for someone to drown in a riptide?

These currents develop close to the shore and take people out to sea. What's so disarming is that riptides look calm from the surface, especially as they will have waves on either side of them. Now, if you're looking at your team from your vision (the beach) of what things are supposed to be, you are living a dream, they're drowning.

So, leadership, relationships, mentoring, coaching, emotional intelligence, and change are all needed to build up our people. The other important aspect of the workplace is company culture, as it will reinforce all that you give to them. When you take a day off it's the culture of the company that will maintain what you've put in place.

I had to write this book because of the loneliness, frustration, desperation, and hopelessness I felt in my own difficult situations. And, I see others that are still in theirs. Situations that they should be well able and equipped to handle. We need a persistent and consistent program to assess and address the well being of our people. Leadership is not on-demand, it is always in demand.

Who's leading whom? Are you leading your ego or is your ego leading you?

I am not a theologian but allow me the indulgence of making a comparison. In the beginning, God established what I call the *Continuity of Leadership*. He created Adam and gave him dominion of the garden. Adam, for his part became anti-leadership when he decided to go against God's will to do something that would benefit him. Adam was so new to leadership that his vision was the purpose given to him by God, the garden - it happens that way. When we gain more experience, we create a vision that supports our bosses' vision.

But, Adam turned from the vision, or purpose, of caring for the garden, and instead he allowed self/ego to rule him. He lined us up with a new continuity of leadership. I used all lower-case letter here because this new line is false. In fact, I'd like to refer to it as a *Decay Chain*. In Nuclear Science, a decay chain consisting of radioisotopes undergo a process of decay, and then create a new generation the same as the original. This process will repeat itself, essentially continuing that process.

This is not what God intended, a new line of leadership, and for that line to perpetuate itself. You must ask yourself this question: why it was important for Adam and Eve to gain the knowledge of good and evil if they lived in a garden paradise? What would they do with it? So, the premise was only about Adam and Eve gaining something for self/ego. There was no benefit for the purpose given to them.

Do you see how wrong it is to lead people to your ego? He had one job!

The by-product of being led by your ego is at some point in the future you'll have to expend more energy defending your office, or position, than running it.

Now, I wouldn't say that Eve wasn't capable of leading – after all she was Adam's helpmeet and literally a part of him.

But, Adam wasn't supposed to follow her. *The Continuity of Leadership* was changed as it was cut off from God. It was now pushed from the serpent's ego to Eve's ego to Adam's ego. For the leader, self/ego is anti-leadership.

All leaders hold a vision. A part of God's vision for the first family was the Garden. When He asked Adam, "Where are you?" it wasn't that God didn't know the physical place that Adam was, I believe he was asking Adam, "Where are you in relation to my vision?"

If you are a leader and in the *Continuity of Leadership*, by default, you're a part of someone's vision. If you stay outside of that continuity, you're in the void – at risk of decaying, and perpetuating that decay.

I'll use this analogy; they were the only people in the garden. They must have stood out just as lights stand out in the night sky. Leaders are like those lights, surrounded by darkness, uncertainty, confusion, lack, and, of course, no vision. Makes sense because there are more followers than leaders.

Light and leadership will dispel darkness, and like the light that we see, leadership has borders because leaders have limitations. Some people incorrectly hypothesize that darkness can move at the same speed of light because as light passes away from a place, darkness moves in just as quickly to fill that space. But, darkness has no mass and cannot be measured. Similarly, you can't measure confusion, lack of direction, or lack of vision.

Gentle Reminder: Lead Your Purpose – Manage Your Principles.

This is one of my biggest themes. Purpose is what you're hired to do. And principles are how we feel about the work we do. Someone argued the point with me and said that his principles drive him to do a good job, and so his purpose and his principles are one and the same.

Let's look at the theme this way: purpose will rarely change, but principles on the other hand can change twice daily – our feelings can change just that quickly. Now, as far as your purpose, your job – you can get additional tasks to do, but this is not a new job for you.

Put it this way, as time goes on, your purpose can remain the same. Given the same period, your principles face a 95% chance of changing. I know this because few people will say, "You know, this job just keeps getting better each day!" Those are your principles.

This second book was supposed to be continued from the work of the first book, only with a different title, but recent events in my life steered the project in this direction. Not that this is a bad thing, just a different thing. Well, while I was wrapping up the first book, I was still an Assistant Director until that company lost its contract. It took some months to find the right employment opportunity – longer than I had hoped for.

While writing the first book, I made a spoken word track. Its design was to uplift those who felt pushed down. I was experiencing a noticeable following and I wanted another way to connect with them. I had no idea those very words of comfort that I wrote for others would come back to bring me comfort. Whoever wrote the proposal for my last job's contract, that we ultimately lost – you had one job!

Like I said, I had to get another job, but the new job wasn't in a leadership position and it didn't come with the same salary that I felt I needed to support the quality of life I had become accustomed to. I was starting over again. This new job offered me the shortest commute to work I ever had, and this was desirable, considering the last position was a two-hour commute. I was now a job readiness facilitator, helping people to prepare for, and secure, employment. Let me pause here to share the spoken word track, not for effect but for reference. I'll continue with leadership after this.

This is Shawn Abrams with a message for you and those you lead. 2018 was an eventful year. Like you, I lost some things in this year. I watched as one thing of significant importance to me fell to the ground, but rather that sit at the base of the rubble, I climbed to the top of it to get a better view of the field.

From that point, I realized my sorrow would only subside when I decided that a pause for a failed plan is not a place for mourning, but a place for staging a comeback.

If you felt, or continue to feel, loss and have only committed to recovering someday, know that if you are waiting for the right time, you've waited too long. The inception of your vision will mark the start of your labor. If not, it is only a dream.

Leaders don't dream, they hold a vision. Note the difference between dreams and visions. Dreams are magical places with magical things that cannot exist. Visions are grounded, even if it be in the future. Take comfort in the fact that your vision cannot betray you. It will exist in its time until you bring it to pass.

At the time of this recording there is still time to execute in 2018, or at the very least, to plan to execute. If 2019 is when you plan to strike, take careful aim not to miss your intended targets. Don't listen to naysayers. Anyone who would listen to a voice of dissension is not a leader, but a follower.

This holiday season let's lead those within our sphere of influence to recall what we gained, what we are grateful for, what we have left, and how we made it this far. As a leader you are a part of the very fabric that holds the world together. What you did this year counts for this year and many more to come.

It did well in SoundCloud and I was happy with it. I had soft music playing and everything. I thought it was good!

How prophetic was this? Standing on top of the rubble of what I had built...powerful stuff right there.

Shawn Abrams

Gentle Reminder: A situation is something you can get into. A condition is something that can get inside of you. And, we have little control of it.

Well, in 2019 I found myself once again, standing on top of a rubble, and looking out over the playing field. Sure, it's hard starting over. I resolved the situation because this was a situation not a condition, I'll get to that later.

Lesson: you don't have to think the way you feel. I want my feelings and thoughts shared – the same relationship of church and state. Not necessarily at war with each other, they have the appearance of separate, but equal – they influence each other, but they are separate.

So, if I'm unhappy, I want to think positive thoughts. I have this vision of what is to be and the reality of what is. If our feelings and thoughts are in league with each other. If we think our feelings and thoughts are one and the same, we can get caught in a Twix loop. You know, where you have left Twix and right Twix. We think they're separate because there are two of them, yet we favor one side – no, they're the same.

Okay, enough talk about confections. Let's explore the *Seven Epaulettes of Leadership*, which is about more than leadership – it also explores personal and professional relationships, your vision of the future, your relationship to that vision, and emotional intelligence.

Why do we need a book like this? Well, most of my adult life has been spent leading teams of people. I've worked with people on public assistance, disabilities, youth, prisoners, ex-offenders, and soldiers. My work took me to prisons like Riker's Island, homeless shelters, and various workforce development programs.

The two things that I identified as missing or lacking in the lives of the people I served are strong leadership and strong relationships. Some people weren't leading themselves. They would empower me to lead them, for them.

Leadership is not telling other people what to do and relationships don't work by virtue of your commitment to them.

Leadership is a discipline for the leader. However, you lead people with *Applied Leadership* techniques. In this book, I identify those qualities that leaders and relationships need to be successful.

Adam was given a leadership position and he was put into a relationship with Eve. As I stated earlier, leadership is not telling someone what to do – it can be influence, such as the way Eve influenced Adam. Had Adam recognized leadership as a discipline, he would have seen how the suggestion made to him didn't line up with his boss's vision.

What's interesting to note is that there is no recorded mention of Adam's vision. I'll cover this later, but your vision is to bring all the resources at your disposal and skill you develop through experiences to support your boss's vision.

In his case, I want the knowledge of good and evil so that I can be like a God. Hold that thought while we read through this book in a linear fashion, but you'll have to conceptualize the themes in three dimensions because they often play out simultaneously.

60% of Americans are employed. Over 45% are single. Since relationship dynamics and principles are the same, it's highly likely that some of those single people are on your team. I'm sure some of those single people prefer to be single. But, what about those who don't want to be single and are not good with personal relationships?

Again, some of them may be on your team. This doesn't account for those people who are with someone and they're unhappy with the one they have. How many times have you heard someone speaking loudly or aggressively on the phone to their significant other? Well, you already know they're on your team.

If you're in a leadership position. Take the time to study leadership and relationships, not just for you but for your people – it's a quality of life thing.

I don't expect you to use all the concepts and methodologies I present, but you should use what resonates with you and/or your situation. This book is full of possibilities just like you are. At times, you will be confronted with searing truths and inspiring options for leadership and relationships.

Table of Contents

Ergo Ego

Adam and Eve had purpose, but how do we define that?

P urpose is responsibility and expectation given to us by someone else in exchange for equity which can be laborious or intellectual. We see this at work, where we were hired to do a job. Purpose, as it relates to a job, is explained to us by our employer in the form of a job description. The archenemy for *Purpose* is our *Principles*. We develop the latter while pursuing our purpose.

Principles are our feelings – it's how we feel about the work, the people we work with, and the people we work for. Principles don't exclusively come from our ego, but they also come from our experiences.

Now, let's say a certain person came into their adulthood with some 'self' issues that affected their ego, and the same person had a set of experiences in their previous employment that caused them to develop a set of principles that were not advantageous for work on your team – how do you work all that out?

Do you see how just telling people what to do is not leadership? Managers and supervisors will become frustrated because their much talking will not change the person. In every case like this, it's the manager or supervisor that should change. They must submit to leadership for themselves, and then use *Applied Leadership* to lead their direct reports by coaching and mentoring them.

I've dedicated most of my adult life to helping and leading others. During this time, I've dealt with my own traumatic issues and that of countless others. I had to learn to lead people despite trauma and produce measurable results.

You know how they say, "You can lead a horse to water, but you can't make him drink," This is true, but if a horse is ill it will not drink water no matter how much it needs it. People can get so sick emotionally that they don't take care of themselves the way that they should. How do you lead that person if they work with you or live in your home?

What's an Epaulette?

An epaulette is something that denotes position and rank. It's the fancy material that is worn on a military or quasi-military uniform, usually on the shoulder. Additionally, it can to some extent, denote the responsibilities of the wearer. In a similar fashion, what we believe about ourselves should also be carried by us.

If you believe you are an honorable person, you will conduct yourself that way. If you can earn an epaulette, carry it, and define it, you should be able to impart it to others. Nonetheless, the identifiers should be just as visible. Not as a chip or a trophy, but they should be a part of us. It is a distinct service mark that distinguishes you and what you belong to.

And so, the epaulettes in this book should be taken to be your own. They're designed to be incorporated into you and what you do. It's also in keeping with the importance of the naming conventions that I share with you throughout this book.

Epaulettes we've earned, or desire to earn, will affect how we think. As human beings, what we think and what we feel is important. As professionals, we learned to separate our thoughts and feelings.

Example: we may feel anger, but we understand that angry thoughts are not productive. What we produce out of anger will be born of anger.

The ego for a leader can make them operate under an autarky mindset. That is, willfully independent of anything – in this example, vision. This leader is the sole proprietor and benefactor of what they see and believe. The people simply become an extension of their egos.

Leaders are not cursed, but they face the curse. How often do leaders – business, political, and entertainment leaders, have lost their positions due to themselves? And, usually it's some kind of scandal too – something they could have easily and legally attained with, or without, their leadership positions.

Ego thirsts too, it can never be satisfied. Take Idi Amin, former dictator of Uganda. He ascended the ranks from being a cook in the army to the leader and butcher of his nation. Before he was done, hundreds of thousands of his people were murdered. Prior to his exile from his country, he bestowed himself with a dozen titles.

Ego will drive you to do this. He declared his title to be His Excellency President for Life, Field Marshall Alhaji Dr. Adi Amin Dada, VC DSO, MC, CBE, Lord of all Beasts of the Earth and Fishes of the Sea. So, for some people, simply leading is not enough. Adam, Eve, and Idi were all led by their egos, and consequently, they incurred irreversible consequences. Read on.

Ego is your self-esteem and self-importance. Perceiving one's self as having low self-importance or carrying low self-esteem can enact powerful feelings to compensate for this.

Before this is over you will think I cover feelings a lot, and I do, because our feelings often get us into trouble. Most people can't separate their feelings from their thoughts. And since our feelings often fuel our thoughts, we'll need to explore this.

If you can get people to feel good, they will be thinking good thoughts. You may have purchased this book because it made you feel something. The feeling to buy translated into an impulse to buy. Satisfying, right?

You see, when our thinking and our feelings are aligned, we experience a sense of completion. Notice I said align, not mirror. I feel angry and I think angry thoughts. I would be at odds with myself if felt angry and thought peaceful thoughts. So many people have had the satisfaction of this alignment, the Hatfield's, the McCoy's, the Middle East, gangs, professional skaters, etc. When we think what we feel, which is human, we make a path to our ego.

We try to suppress our feelings so we can be led by our higher thinking. Military indoctrination requires fighting persons to follow lawful orders without question. They seem indifferent when they execute the duties and we like this about them. We need to know that they will follow lawful orders, and not let their feelings cloud their judgment.

Some prisoners understand this and have a similar regimen for their ranks. Some prisoners even take cold showers in order to adapt to shock. This way, they can better mask their emotions in the face of danger or physical attack. This is controlling one's self so that you can respond, and not react, to situations.

But, how do you do this for your office workers? You can't make them take cold showers, march them, or make them sing songs. There's no blood in, blood out. These people don't fear their leadership. And, if it's a union shop forget it!

For the record, I have nothing against unions, but if there is a union worker that moves as slow as a tortoise, and the union acted as a shell for that worker, you would never motivate them, or otherwise get to them.

In New York, right now, the public transportation system paid more than one billion US dollars in overtime for work that isn't even done. One worker earned more in overtime than the mayor and governor earned, combined! The service is often delayed, capital projects are overrun in costs, and some services were cut. The service has people in leadership positions, but where's the leadership?

Mark my words: Whenever there is a systemic problem in an organization, the problem is leadership!

Workers will do what they're allowed to do! If you utilize *Applied Leadership* for your subordinate leaders, and they do the same for their subordinate leaders, and so on and so on, until you reach the lowest ranking staff, you will achieve what the military possesses in its fighting men and women. This is the problem for some organizations. There is no systematic way to pass on leadership training.

Note: Unions are an important part of American life and quality of life, without them we would have widespread worker unrest, police would have a difficult time keeping order, and workers would be taken advantage of. It seems like there is no happy middle ground.

An honest leader will see that they may not be the best coaches or mentors. This is okay as long as they can identify someone who is there to help them. Don't assume that your subordinate leaders are good or good enough – how do you know?

Give all your leaders a test and find out what they think leadership is. Ask them to describe their leadership style.

Ask them:

- Are they teaching leadership to their staff?
- If so, what doctrine are they following?
- How do they evaluate themselves, and others, as leaders?
- How do they gauge how well the staff is 'training up' in just leadership?

If you're not doing this and you don't know the answers to these questions, you have a break in the *Continuity of Leadership* in your organization. I'm sure you'll get some lip service from some and silent honesty from others, but when you find the gap, bridge it!

You think the people farthest away from you are happy because they have a job and you hear success stories, but you may only be leading the upper echelon of your organization. If you have initials in front of your title and after your name at the same time, make it your business to check your continuity, be sure you lead all the people.

While writing this book, I felt like I needed a visual to represent the project. The "Work Love – Love Work" logo was a concept I thought about for a few weeks until I could get it to a graphic artist. I want people to love what they do for leadership and relationships. Everyone we engage with may not want, or be able, to reciprocate these feelings, but I believe you reap what you sow. And, it's your brand. You will be known for what you do and what you don't do.

The Seven Epaulettes of Leadership was conceived to be a close-quarter utilitarian companion for the success of those who dare to lead.

Ego Powers Revenge

Warfare, it seems, is born out of revenge. The events that led up to WWI began with the assassination of Archduke Franz Ferdinand. Sure, there were tensions before this, but his death set the chain of events that led to the war. The U.S. did not enter WWII until the Japanese bombed Pearl Harbor. Most recently, there is a war on terrorism. That was revenge for 911.

America has been in many wars, but make no mistake about it, America's longest war is not the war on terror, it's the war of tribal politics. We see the weaponization of leadership in politics. Don't think that because you don't subscribe to a tribe that you can sit it out. If you fit a demographic, you're assigned to a tribe.

Ego Powers Purpose?

What is the secret of life? It's simple – it's to live. So, whose idea was it to begin a journey to look for the journey? It's like a martial arts student that spends his life training and seeking a *master* to teach him the highest level of martial arts there is. The master tells this dedicated student, "The highest form of marital arts is not to fight at all!" Seriously, that's where you started, right? I get it, it's the journey that gave this person purpose, but this is not right thinking.

If you knew you had purpose in the beginning, what would you have done? I think what these students are missing is, you don't find purpose, you discover it. If you're trying to find it, you're trying to create it. This is not purpose – this is a hobby. Your sense of self-worth (ego) wants to find validation, a reason for living.

If you're in a leadership position, a part of your purpose, as it relates to that position, is to develop the epaulettes and character traits in the people you lead to sustain their purpose. You don't necessarily need to know what that is. Before you lead anyone, you firstly lead yourself. Pass this on to them so they will lead themselves to their purpose.

I know, the leader they had before you should have done this – it's their fault, but it's your problem to correct. If you said to yourself, "No one else could have done this for them, it's my job!" – you're in that leadership space. Now, let's find out where we are so that we can know where we're going.

Situational Awareness II

If you had a heads-up display for your life what would be on your screen right now?

This is one of my favorite terms – *Situational Awareness*. I need information to make decisions and in this information age, we have access to know all kinds of things at a moment's notice. But what information do you concern yourself with right now and what information is overlaid onto your vision of the future?

Heads up displays are a great convenience for hands free flying or driving. Pilots and drivers have so many things going at any given time it's easy to get distracted by non-actionable information. We may be doing too many things while we should be paying attention, but that's beside the point.

If I lived a sedentary life and carried all the information I have now, I could handle that. But, I'm always moving and thinking, even when I'm at rest. Additionally, situations change often. Let's consider our vision of the future. What real-time information do we need to make decisions?

Metrics are often concerned with how many, how much, how quick, how long, and comparisons. But, how many companies include team morale and quality of life initiatives? I guess we don't want these factors to become excuses if we're not doing well.

If the leader's vision is the big picture, then the operation's vision is concerned with the pixels and the big picture. It's rare to find people that can see their vision and all the things necessary for their vision in real-time.

I can come up with extremely complex goals, but I have a difficult time with the details. Seeing up close causes me to slow down and focus. It sounds like slowing down is a good thing, but after spending time seeing far off, (figuratively), I become impatient with the details. I find people who are good with operations are those detail people. They concern themselves with policy and exactness. Nothing wrong with this, but for me to succeed, I need someone like that to work with.

After leadership, operations is the most important concern of an organization. They literally connect the dots. They never, ever lose sight of the picture. They must know how and where each pixel fits into the picture.

Applied Leadership is targeted to the human capital of your organization – both staff and customers.

Leadership, in general, affects the feelings of people. To quote the urban vernacular, "You feel me?"

Operations targets the thought processes of people. It is concerned with logistics, planning, execution, audits, control, supportive branding, timelines, morale, sobering reality, and policy.

Some companies go wrong when they mistakenly believe that leadership alone will cover the above listed practice areas. There must be a central point that has access to data to make recommendations and internal decisions in order maintain quality of life for workers and profit margins for investors. The absence of this role or department will allow confusion and frustration to exceed production.

Workers will begrudgingly do their jobs, they may call out of work a lot, customer complaints may increase, and loss of human capital will occur.

Why are we surprised that we ran out of copy paper? Why did we allow the workers to amass vacation days, and then suffer through mass vacations prior to the end of the fiscal year? Why will we struggle with environmental controls? I've worked in a lot of companies where the environmental controls were adjusted multiple times in a day because the workers were split on how warm or cool the office should be.

In many cases, companies *wait* for first-line supervisors to report poor performance of a worker. If the supervisor decides to issue corrective action for the worker,

Human Resources will want:

- An unbiased view of that person's performance
- A sample of someone that is performing
- The job description
- And the policy as it relates to the shortcoming

It should be operations monitoring production, and then informing Human Resources that corrective actions, possibly employment relationship decisions, may need to be made. This way, it's no surprise when these situations are rolled up to them.

Operations can suggest that a review of *Best Practices of High Performers* be shared with those that are struggling.

All this can take a long time to resolve. And, all the while, profit is being lost. Therefore, it is advantageous to lead the worker out of poor performance. Ideally, the leader would have mentored and coached the worker to avoid this in the first place. I know, it's not easy, but this is what you signed on for when you decided to be a leader.

Why do we even need a book on leadership and relationships? Well, some of our problems we have are centered on relationships with people or things. A poor relationship with money can have the same effect that a poor relationship with a person can have.

Bob Ross School of Conflict Resolution

How often do we take time out to assess the well being of our teams? People hold back all kinds of stuff that gets in the way of work.

Conflict Resolution – There should be a Bob Ross school of conflict resolution. Remember Bob Ross, the painter? He was the white guy with the Afro that painted beautiful paintings in thirty minutes with a cool calm that made you forget everything.

His school should be in a studio with dozens of students eager to learn the Bob Ross method of conflict resolution. Students should learn how to talk like him. They would learn how to control a situation as easily as Bob can control his palette. And they should apply their solutions as easily as Bob could apply his paint strokes to his canvas.

Imagine, two people at odds in the workplace. The Bob Ross resolution specialist would come over and erase the source of contention, calmly repeat everything each party says, and then repaint the scene to a tranquil setting.

Gentle Reminder: Leaders are born in and raised out of trouble.

You're not a referee or a judge, don't arrive at the solution before the other parties involved. It's like getting to a party too early or on time. There's no one else there with you. Sure, you did the right thing, but you're weird because you're early.

The thing to remember is conflict is normal. We can coach the emotions of all parties involved, to the extent that they will allow it. Well, if they are on your team, you can assure them that their feelings matter, their opinions count for something, and you can point out any similarities that they share.

But, under no circumstance will we take a side or declare a winner or the one will love you and the other will hate you. These situations must end in a draw because if anyone loses on your team your whole team loses. There is only excellence and consequence.

What if the conflict is with the leader? Yikes!

Just because we are in a leadership position doesn't mean we're right! I just wanted to start with that. Not everyone holds their leader in high regard. Unfortunate, but some have an "us against them" attitude. We don't want to give the appearance that we are above reproach or above our people.

Some staff have disliked a new supervisor before they even met him or her. If you take it personal, your ego will lead you away from your purpose and right into your principles. I've said this a few times, "Purpose is our job and our principles are what we develop in the course of doing our jobs."

You can't fight your team and you don't want them to fight your leadership. If it's true that leadership is a discipline for me, the leader, then I'll need to protect it from my ego.

Devalued relationships, you may have heard me say this before: I don't want respect, I don't try to earn respect, and I don't lose sleep over not gaining respect.

This is because people will give you respect when they like you, and when they stop liking you, they take back their respect. I don't want anything that you can give to me, and then take away if you get upset with me. I've learned that nice guys do finish last. That is, if you are trying to be nice you will be taken advantage of. Instead, I prefer to be fair.

You may not like me, you may not respect me, but you will respect fair!

Leaders don't nest in their problems – they lead people out of the nests they build for themselves in their difficult situations. To nest in a situation is to extend your time there. It is to make the uncomfortable tolerable. Initially this is okay as we all do this.

We lick our wounds, assess the situation, complain about the situation, and look for others in a similar situation because it makes us feel good to know that this didn't just happen to us.

A natural response to trauma is to settle yourself, try to alleviate the distress, try to feel better, and then find comfort. Right there, the last part. There's nothing wrong with finding comfort, but once you start it's hard to stop until just about every chance we get we try to continue finding comfort.

Soon, it will be difficult to leave the situation due to all the resources and energy expended. This is the beginning of the nest.

Gentle Reminder: Don't nest in your situation.

A nest is a comfortable pattern we subscribe to. It becomes our internal culture, it placates our ego, and it safeguards us from the 'un's' that is the:

- unfamiliar
- uncomfortable
- unmatchable
- unbearable
- unprecedented
- unconventional, etc.

Things happen, I get it. There are situations we find ourselves in, sometimes at no fault of our own, that we cannot easily get out of. But, it's human nature to try and find comfort at that time. Going through something is not so bad if someone else is too. And we begin nesting. We pull in anyone and anything that will bring us comfort.

This is also known as a comfort zone. The problem with this is your nest is built for comfort because you put things in it to make you comfortable, not successful.

Think about the people you keep close to you. Are they supporting the maintenance of your nest, or are they trying to get you to leave it? Please don't think you can have your cake and eat it too. You can't stay in your nest and have success!

So, this nest that we all create, which is natural, can become a death trap. At first it will protect our ego, then cover it, then shield it, and then block it. Leaders don't necessarily have this problem, but they need to understand that many of those they lead or serve do.

Now, we have another angle to explore. Some companies can create death traps for their employees. Yes, employers can build nests too. Due the size of the enterprise, the size of the nest could be substantial. You could conceivably build a Hotel California in Coolio's Gangstas Paradise.

These are not just places with a physical address of longitude and latitude, it's a mindset, and it's the culture. We promote people we're comfortable with and we hire people who are well within the six degrees of separation.

People visit with the intention to stay awhile, but they don't leave. The average worker is comprised of more than just work. There are two parts to the worker – the work and the 'er.' The (er) is a suffix, it's an actual person. The mistake here is treating the worker, but not as a person.

We get busy and we think this is productive in and of itself. And so, it will be hard to move people out, onto their next employer, hard to move people upward, and hard to identify real issues. Workers will only leave this nest for an offer to go to another one. Notice I said another one because they've become accustomed to the nest.

When they do leave, it's for a promotion or more money, exactly what your nest didn't offer. Perhaps they could have stayed longer if there was a culture that was advantageous for them. One that included actual training from someone at the unit level.

Okay, we see the importance of the (er) suffix. Let's look at the (ship) suffix part of leadership. In the next chapter, I explain how leadership is a discipline for you, the leader. Right now, we'll dissect the work and focus on the (ship) part of the word which means character. Therefore it's you, not the people you lead. More on that in the next chapter as well.

I taught Job Readiness classes and found that the culture of each class was different, although, the teaching I gave them was the same. I couldn't duplicate what I had the first time around. Each class had its own identity. Success for them and me depended on my ability to respect each team's collective personality while setting the tone for them. Before I can lead people to success, I need to have success.

Succeeding in the First Person

How do you measure success, with a yardstick or a surveyor's wheel?

I prefer my success to be long and great. I can't use small units of measurement or small tools to measure my success. I'm not talking about goals – I can set a series of small goals. Yardstick thinking will put me in the company of people that won't challenge me. I would feel good because I am like a king in this company.

Here's the yardstick: it's safe, it's comfortable, it requires little effort on my part, it's easily attained, and I hold a sense of accomplishment.

Now, there are times when we can set small goals as practice for larger ones, but I'm beyond that now. I don't need comfort – I need a challenge! I can't grow bigger in the same space. I can begin the process of leading myself – by coaching myself, and then find someone to mentor me – that would be cool! The mentor would see me as less work for them.

Mentor's don't use yardsticks to measure their mentee's. Additionally, I can find others, like me, that have or are being coached because fortunately there are many coaches. I think a lot of self-help books are written by coaches, or the coaching type of person – this is fine by me.

Do you know many people are totally against self-help books? In fact, the genre doesn't attract people to review these books even if they did read them. Coaches inspire you to be greater, but mentors expect you to be greater, and they're not so common. Not everyone wants to share the secret sauce.

The mentor is not the person who teaches professional development classes, that's the coach, but a mentor can be that same person – it's what they call you to do outside of that class that's mentoring.

Yardstick thinking has a quick goal and a quick vision. I'm not opposed to this, but anything we obtain quickly can leave quickly. Imagine that quick vision becoming a blur because it came and went too fast. This may be why so many lottery winners lose it all in a short span of time. Yes, I do fall into the self-help area, a little bit.

This chapter was intended to be included in the follow up to my first book. And this was the perfect title: *Succeeding in the First Person*. I might come back to that project someday, but for now, I want to explore more of what *The Seven Epaulette's of Leadership* has to offer as it is a more concise look at leadership and relationships.

I made an abecedarian mistake during the writing of the first. The production was on a timeline with set goals, but I didn't have fun with it. I made what was to be a good work, well, work. I seldom enjoyed myself as I was so focused on completing the book, and I shouldered all the creative and logistical processes. This time, I'm going to have fun and enjoy myself. The book hadn't sold a copy of yet, I was still writing it, but I felt success.

I like to ask my new team members how they define success. I can get as many different answers as there are people in the room. This is good and bad, as what's important to you may not be important to anyone else. This is a situation for a leader to address. Your vision must be shared, and you can offer to assist them with their vision of how they can do their part. How can you help someone to feel like they have success if you don't know how they define success?

For a team the opposite of success is not failure, it's poor leadership. Failure is simply the byproduct of poor leadership. Look at your team. Are they seemingly taking turns calling out of work? That's no different than being married but working late to avoid going home. We check out of relationships when they are not fulfilling. We let relationships degrade because we haven't learned self-emotional maintenance and repair.

If we can't do this for ourselves, we can't do this for others. Put in the work, challenges will come. Having load-bearing discussions now about our feelings will nicely shoulder the weight of relationship issues. Sure, the conversations may not be comfortable, but at least they won't be brought on by someone's triggers.

You can't be comfortable and successful at the same time.

Supervisors can be good at solving problems. What would be great is if they could see problems before they surface – but seeing the problem first doesn't make you a leader. It's the plan you develop to address this. It's coaching and mentoring your team to handle the stress, uncertainty, limitations, contingencies, and facilitating quality of life measures to keep them going.

You came to the future, you saw the future, and you conquered the future before your team made it to the future because you are their leader. If you do this as a practice, your team will begin to do this too. They will see some of what's coming that you may not see. All kinds of good things can come out of this. Like, they may not schedule time off during the period that they believe will require them to be present. They might see that a real-time project's end date will collide with this future event and decide to complete it early to accommodate for it.

While the brain is involved with the process of us feeling pain, it cannot feel pain itself. This is because it has no pain receptors in or on it. Headaches don't take place in your brain. We should be glad for this. Imagine a world where someone driving could experience pain in their brain, important sections of the brain would become compromised.

So, there is a relationship between the brain and the body, but there is also a disconnect between the two. When I talk to people that have taken some drastic measure that they regret, I ask them, "Do you have to think the way you feel?" It's a loaded question, but I need to make the comparison. I want them to see the thinking what we feel can make us go too far. Sure, it's human, but it's not professional.

The police officer faces someone with a gun aimed at them. They may feel anger and fear. Their survival instinct may push them to use a measure of force that would result in an irreversible act, but they know that the preferred method is to talk the person down. Not everyone can separate their feelings from their thinking. First responders are trained to do this. They may feel fear, but they have to do a job despite that. They have to think about the successful outcomes that they want, not the fear that they have.

I like to ask people if their work is limited to their abilities or their feelings. Now, they'll argue either side, but I want to explore the consequence of their choice. Your abilities generally don't degrade, (all things being equal), but, our emotional state can, and it can degrade in a short amount of time based on how we feel. I'm not saying we must always deny self, but our profession, a situation, or an expectation may require us to prioritize the expectation of our abilities above and beyond our feelings.

You can learn something from the boss. The word *boss* come from the Dutch word *master*. Both words carry a stigma, but this would also imply that the boss has mastered work up to the point of their official title, whatever that may be.

It is important to note that while you may not be particularly fond of your boss, you can learn from this person. If you let your ego, or their ego, get in the way of your growth, you would never attain the level they have. Children learn through imitation and adults learn through experience and studying.

Your vision is to support your boss's vision.

This level is higher than other levels. You have the same weapons and tactics at your disposal, but the threat is greater. Up to this point, the game coached you with rewards and the satisfaction of advancement. They represented promotion through effort and now, all that you learned has come to a culmination of game play on the *boss* level.

What typically happens when you best this boss, is you begin the next level in the game. Cool, right? But, no game allows you to beat the boss and become the new boss. I guess this is because the boss is portrayed as an evil character. I wish there was a game where you became a game boss and faced against other players.

The boss is the mentor archetype. This is your testing of the pseudo coaching stages. And so, your boss is necessary for your growth. I'm quite sure truly mentored know this, but do all bosses know this too? Do all bosses know that in order to get the best out of their team they have to grow them?

How do you coach and mentor your subordinate leader(s) to coach and mentor their direct reports? I would draw on my boss's experience as they would have likely faced the same situation, and this helps to keep the integrity of the CLC.

Since every organization will lose employees to attrition, they'll have to have a robust leadership training program in place to replace leaders. No disrespect to workers, but they are easier to find than leaders. Now, if you can't, or won't, pay a competitive wage, expect people to gain experience, and then move on.

Leadership can help to keep people a little longer as they will see that what they gain is useful for their careers. They will eventually leave, but what you will have is a shop of people who can accept leadership and exert some measure of it over themselves and others. Any new worker will fall in line with the culture of the shop, and so the cycle becomes easier to manage. Of course, as the responsibilities increase, so should the training.

Coaching can become addictive for the person administering the coaching, and the person receiving it, which is why we must move the person being coached to mentoring. This is the goal.

Leaders should not try to make a forever team. If you care for people, and you have success, some of them will want to be like you. They will want to do what you do, which may result in them moving on.

Gentle Reminder: You can't have success and comfort at the same time.

You know you're doing your job right when they're doing their job right. But how do we pass this on – what is leadership?

Leadership II

Leadership is a discipline for you, the leader, not the people you lead.

When I ask groups of people what's the difference between a manager and a leader, they always describe the leader as a more important role, yet they struggle to define what a leader is.

Words like lead, leader, and leadership carry a stigma with them. I think, therefore, some people in leadership positions shy away from its pure form and embrace manager and management. It is what it is, use it.

If you're just a manager, you're the protagonist and antagonist to your story. Your end is the beginning and you don't get to write your story – you just get to live it.

Companies don't typically train employees for leadership. They try to find people with leadership qualities or experience. A leadership program is not as expensive as some may think. Not compared to what you stand to lose if you have ineffective leaders in place.

I help people gain self-sufficiency by helping them to obtain employment. I tell them that I intend to lead them from day one through their first job after class completion. I add the disclaimer that I am by no means better than them. It's just my job to lead them during this period of their lives, as it relates to employment. I explain the breakdown of leadership the way I did in the opening of this chapter.

Being new to each other, I must coach them, as they may be shy, apprehensive, or received poor coaching in the past. And, I tell them they will need to interact with others that they don't know during the training. I need them to become a cohesive group. I want to encourage them, I let them know mistakes are not punishable, but in life there is excellence and consequence.

There is much technical work to do while coaching. I need get their expectations and share my own. I need to uncover patterns that will not support success. The period to do this will vary with the individual and I must move the entire class corporately in some given areas.

To gauge our ability to succeed, I'll have to leave coaching and enter mentoring. This is not to say that I will never coach them again, but the students will have to "come to me" rather, show me, that they can leave the training/coaching start point. These two mediums, coaching and mentoring, comprise the *Applied Leadership* method.

Say a certain someone is interested getting to know someone else, but the target is reluctant to do so due to previous relationships woes. Some would call those woes baggage and move on. Still others may decide to engage the thinking that there would be less competition, or the target just needs the right someone to come along.

Well, the person pursuing would coach the target by making supportive statements like:

- You're making the right decision, right now!
- You deserve better!
- You didn't lose anything good – you let go of something difficult.
- This will pass, and you will meet new interesting people.
- You can use what you've learned about previous relationships to vet future ones.

There are a host of other statements. You're coaching their emotions because, to the target, it's worse to feel bad than it is to think badly. After some period, the pursuer would ask questions like, "Do you feel better about relationships now?"

This is mentoring as you're trying to see how far the target has come along. When you coached them, you showed them their strength. Now, as the mentor, you're showing them your strength. This is important, as no one will follow a weak mentor.

The mentor needs to possess something worth following. The work that you do in these mediums is not made on the fly. You would have carefully planned this out – to the extent that you can anyway. If the appropriate time and care is put into the endeavor, success may follow.

And, this is how we can lead the target into a relationship. We do this instinctively, but the professional does this consistently. No, I don't mean picking up people, I mean executing the application of *Applied Leadership.*

If you have these issues or shortcomings in your organization, you can work on it, they can be fixed, but this will take some time. However, you need to lead to increase your professional capacity. That is, you will need to have more patience, make more time for coaching, account for a new learning curve, shepherd this transitional process (which may differ from the way you lead the team up to this point), and sell all of it to the team. We will continue to sell the changes to the team by campaigning for the needed changes.

You will feel proud to say, *"The Continuity of Leadership Chain* has been restored, and the dysfunction of yesterday is no more!" And, don't feel sorry for yourself – if everything was fine, they wouldn't need you to lead them.

Professional Capacity

What is professional capacity? It is something that can be measured by one's ability to function according to purpose, without compromise, distress, or loss.

To be more granular, one should be able to lead one's self and those they are charged with leading to their established vision or expected end. To be more accurate, I should not ignore or otherwise lose the ability to lead anyone because I have too many people to lead.

How can we quantify the number of people we can lead? Well, that's not an easy question to answer as it depends on the leader, their experience, the way they lead, the assigned work, and to some extent the people they lead.

Now, that is, with all things being equal. Just because someone led a team of ten doesn't mean they were successful in that endeavor. So, if you're interviewing someone for a leadership position, it is imperative that you inquire about:

- Their leadership style
- If they received formal leadership training
- What condition was the team morale when they started
- And, then when they left
- What motivated the team,
- What did they themselves learn from the team and/or a mentor
- How did they measure success
- How did they take that team to success
- How much time was spent on building the team in comparison to other activities

This is not a comprehensive list, but it should give some insight.

Now, here's the tricky part, you may be looking for someone that matches your style or preference, but how well do you know the team you propose to assign this person to?

What weaknesses does the team have, and how long have they had these weaknesses?

I'll belabor the point about not being able to define what leadership is. This example has us trying to identify the best-fit leader for our team.

If you have many departments and smaller units within them, but no companywide definition of leadership, what would you accomplish? Cui bono?

Let's try to determine the valuation of your *Continuity of Leadership Chain*, hereafter known as CLC.

Ask everyone in your company how they define these three words: leadership, relationship, and success.

If you have 40 people and receive 120 different answers, you have a problem. If the answers are split too many ways you still have a problem, and it depends on how the split occurs. If more than 25% of the staff have different answers, they're not being led, but are most likely being managed.

Let's quantify this statement. If your production levels are acceptable, profits are in the black, employee turnover is low, employee callouts are low, and HR is not reporting a high volume of incidents, you might assume that all is well.

I won't argue with that, from a company standpoint. These metrics don't support themselves, but this is not a natural occurrence. Random events don't produce perfection, success, or prosperity. If the lot you drew produced undesirable results, then you would need to find out why before you could make things right.

Now, all things being equal, let's drill down. We should start at 100% and deduct points for each shortcoming. I'll break this into quarters to make this simple, but you can revise the point system to your liking. If you surveyed all your front-line workers and found that all staff offered clearly misaligned responses, you can deduct 50% off your CLC, as they represent the bulk of customer service and labor.

If somehow, they gave acceptable responses, but your first-line supervisors offered misaligned responses, deduct 25% from your CLC, as they assign the work, lead the staff, and absorb any shortages in staffing.

Now, it's highly unlikely that your director level leaders and above will give far-off responses. They would likely have had some formal leadership training, or would have a good deal of experience in leadership positions, but if just one of them offers and answer that is not close to what you expect, you have an entire practice area of your organization that is cut off from the top.

The base (bottom half) of this structure is the largest at 50%. These people produce the outcomes while the top half produces the strategy. See, half your organization can be cut off from the *Applied Leadership* of the strategy echelon while still interacting with them, daily.

The base, without a clear channel for *Applied Leadership* to flow to them, will make your organization's working *Continuity of Leadership* path a virtual org-chart.

- **25% Customer client**
- **25% Staff**
- **25% First-line Supervisors**
- **25% Director and above**

Applied Leadership works when what the top leadership believes, every level through the customer also believes. And, whatever the customer thinks filters up through all the levels, up to the CEO.

The flow of influence from the CEO must be constant and continuous – without break – in order to influence the emotions of the customer. In return for this, the customer will respond by thinking they are cared for. The CEO is coaching the feelings of all the levels down, which will affect everyone's thinking up. Rather, purchase/loyalty decisions in favor of the company/CEO.

Look at that, 50% of your CLC is spent on the people farthest from the senior leadership. This is where most of your turnover, and shrinkage, occurs. If they are not happy, staff and customers will leave. So, why don't we teach the supervisors leadership and operations to excite and motivate the base level?

This means that everyone above must receive CLC training.

In theory, this method will not end with the customer. If done correctly and consistently, the customer will train those within their sphere of influence.

Nature knows what *time* it is.

The queen bee doesn't replicate herself, nor does she replicate the work, but she does replicate the workers. There are three tiers in the beehive. There is the queen, the workers, and the drones. This is not the most palatable comparison, but you get the idea.

I don't say that customers are drones, but their movements must be drone-like, and only *emotional droning* can do this. People often do what they see others doing – rather, droning.

When companies fail, they scramble to find new ways to do the same work when they should be looking for the right way to use the same people to do the same work. We're not replicating leaders we're replicating the methodology. Believe me, you'll never be able to replicate a great leader.

Imagine, putting your business on top of a dynamic like this. If you have leaders like this in your organization, and you don't have a method by which to teach and prove them, then how do you know they are good leaders?

In my line of work, I lead people, so I wear both the mentor's hat and the coach's hat to teach classes for job seekers. Some of who may not have had an effective coach or a coach at all. My form of coaching must be more supportive and encouraging. Adults have lived their way all their lives. Having someone come along and tell you what to do can be off-putting.

The student must travel to a mentor, and a mentor will expect this. Every movie with a student that wants to be a master will first seek out a master to teach them. The master never travels to the student.

The most recent example of this is in the *Doctor Strange* movie. Dr. Strange wanted to regain normal use of his hands. He travels across the world to meet with the Ancient One. Shortly after their initial encounter, Dr. Strange is thrown out of her sanctuary.

He stays there at her door begging to get in to be taught. Now, the Ancient One knew Dr. Strange had potential and she knew she would teach him, yet she left him to reflect on his early disbelief. Why then did she have him go through the ordeal when she could have just hastened his application process? Well, in my opinion, she allowed him to go through life stuff to prove to himself, not her, that he wanted it.

Mentors will do this: They will demand that the student move from the mental space that they are in. Of course, some students must move physically – the point here is the student moves toward the mentor. A coach by comparison, will move to the student. A coach will meet the student where they are. The mentor will see the life obstacles that the student has, will have, and must traverse to get to them. This is the best part. Despite the obstacles for the student, the mentor will insist that they come to them.

What's so beautiful about this is that the mentor still sees the student despite the obstacles. This should tell the student that they are special, they are recognized, worthy, and equipped for the task.

Before I challenged my students to come to me, I spoke to them early in our relationship about the topic. I would put it this way: Imagine that I am standing in the front of the class in mentor mode and I call forth a student from the back of the room.

They might look at all the desks, laptops and chairs between us. They might complain that there are many people between us. They might fear that some other student will come forward to speak with me before they can. They might fear that I will not wait for them to arrive to where I am, but the situation is clear, if I call you – you must come to me.

You know, some of my students would make it to me and complain that after arriving they have not met their goal. This amazed me because I would have to remind them that making it to me was bigger than the goal, up to that point. If you can make it to me, you surely can make it to the goal on your own.

During their trip to me they had to navigate down an aisle, experience distractions, become overwhelmed with all the activity around them, evaluate easier opportunities, and overcome their doubts.

So, as a mentor I cannot leave my position unattended. Now, if I had to coach that same person, I would make the trip to them. Coaches push you and they say things that make you feel good. You know, they say "You can do it – believe in yourself!" They meet you where you are.

I have no problem wearing both hats, but I believe most people prefer a coach to a mentor because they want to feel good. Let's go back to that example where I met the person where they are. We can collaboratively work on the situation, I can say things that make you feel good, but this is only for a short time. I will have to put back on my mentor hat to move the entire class forward.

Now, if the person asked me a question that I just answered and this was due to insecurities, I have to say as much. After pointing that out I will leave them. Not because I am annoyed, but because I can't stay with them in their insecurities. I would not profit them, it would exhaust me, and it would not leave me enough energy to work with other students.

Do you know what would happen if the other students saw me placating insecurities? They would allow their insecurities to surface as well.

The great thing about being mentored is once the process is complete you can now mentor others. Provided your mentor thinks along the lines of *Continuity of Leadership*, which will find the mentee extremely open to passing to someone else what they themselves have learned.

Examining CLC on a micro level will let me know if my students can follow me from coaching through mentoring for the duration of the class. But, the litmus test is if they follow me after the class is over. Will they take to heart and put into action all they've learned?

There's a lot playing out while we're still in class. I may have to quickly switch from the coaching hat to the mentoring hat to see who is still with me, and sometimes to put distance between myself, and the perceived situation the student is dealing with, but not the person.

This is important as my good intentions can surface the shortcomings that others possess and drown me in what distracts them. In some of these cases, I will say, "I am sorry that you're still processing the feelings and thinking from that time, but they will not serve you for today." We can have a good cry at my desk, but after it's over you still won't have a job.

I then want to point out how they went through life taking care of the things and people that they are responsible for, even though their past is still present. I might ask if it's possible to connect with me until they get what they need just as they've done before. I'll take a soft yes, or a maybe, or even a pause for contemplation, but a hard 'no' would be difficult given that I have others to serve and a timeframe to work within.

I'm also okay with people who walk up to me and say, "You don't understand, I went through so much, I don't think I can do this." I'm okay with this as well. Ambiguity is often the result of a protracted experience that gives rise to negative thinking. If they have the energy reserves to come up to me and say all this, they just want to be heard and they want me to feel something.

I can accommodate because I'm coaching. That makes me smile inside. In fact, they usually go on to coach me by saying something like, "You know people this or people that." If they can speak in generalities as it pertains to their situation, it's a good sign. It could mean that they find comfort in saying they are the average person, and this speaks to why they feel the way they do, but it also means that they can rise above the intimacy of their unique situation.

You have situations in front of you, between you and your mentor. Deal with it and start moving toward them. The mentor can see the difficulties we have, but the fact that they can see us and we can see them means we have to move/act. Coaches will come to us because it's part of their function.

I get it. The coach delivery is more acceptable because we want to hear nice things from them. We also want them to listen to our sad stories and empathize with our situations and conditions. They can help us to maintain the status quo – not that this is a bad thing.

The coach comes to you or your frame of mind. People good at coaching are usually in a close or similar station in life. You might eat lunch with your coach often and see them on a schedule. Whereas a lunch with your mentor is a rare treat. You know that with the mentor you will get some rare golden nugget of information that will change your life, if you dare to apply it.

The mentor mindset can be unforgiving and relentless. I saw this prior to getting promoted to supervisor. I was extremely demanding of my clients. I was trying to get them to meet me where I was. I couldn't balance coaching and mentoring as efficiently as I had for so many years. This revelation is part of what led me to pursue the supervisor position.

My mentor leaning mindset was better suited to supervise others that would directly serve our clients. This is important to note because some of you are there now. It may not be burnout or time to change careers, there may not be anything wrong with the clients, it's just you must move up. If you make the berth of your foundation too wide, you'll end up with a warehouse and not a skyscraper. Don't get me wrong warehouse workers and owners, I love you all, but in this context, we'll end up with a warehouse full of regret.

Our mentors also help us to keep clean the lens, or perspective, of our vision.

Now, just about every leader will have to delegate at some point. Delegation is not a sink or swim proposition. To do so could cost you the trust and confidence of your subordinate. Don't delegate problems. Well, we won't call them problems. They're tasks, that interest the supervisor, but can be addressed by a well-qualified team member.

There is no fail option. The two outcomes available are successful completion or an unintentional lesson.

Selling is Leading

Selling without concern for the buyer is presumptuous. Selling without knowing the buyer is also presumptuous. In order to have success and make a sale in both examples, we need to be concerned and get to know the people we sell to.

Recall me saying: Leadership without the benefit of relationship is bullying. This is how people will perceive

Applied Leadership. Do you see that? *Applied Leadership* will work best if you take time to know people.

Don't think that because they're all professionals and people of a certain age that they will endear themselves to you. I remember a scene in the movie *Training Day* where Denzel's character asked for a gun. A gang member stepped forward, but placed the gun on the ground. He told Denzel that he had to put his own work in.

This is true about real life, if people don't like you, they won't be moved by your authority alone. Sometimes they will make you work and they will watch you work. Get to know people, as this is the foundation of relationships. Chat your people up – inquire about things that concern them.

Remember what they tell you and let them know that you remember and that they are important.

Yes, this is like campaigning! You can relax the effort from time to time, but you will continue to do this indefinitely. When you stop maintaining the relationship it will devolve into an association, and there's no loyalty here.

Devolved relationships are worse than no relationship. At least in the case of the latter, there is no history and what you propose is new and fresh. A devolved relationship puts the leader in a precarious position. People will feel like you've only come around because you need them. If you need a relationship you need to feed a relationship!

Now, your subordinate leaders can have their own leadership style. That is, they can have a unique way of delivering *Applied Leadership*, but this must coach, mentor, and sell to their teams. This is non-negotiable. It's like you're franchising to them. Colonel Sanders pulled franchise licenses from franchisee's that deviated from the formula. And, this is what you will figuratively do for those that try to free style leadership. You can't make this up!

Work alongside them when you can. Show them that you are not too good to do the work that you ask them to do – this too is sales.

Successful leaders sell something that no one else has, or can, sell successfully. And, that my friend is you. If you know what your people want, you can sell to them. You can show them how things they want ties into your vision.

Rally your team around you, not your goal.

No leader can relax their standard and expect those that follow them to maintain theirs. I like this analogy of a staff – which can be a stick or a group of people. A staff is just a stick until you purpose it. At the top of a staff is a flag. It has symbolism and meaning, its strength is in its hoisted position.

Somehow it just won't have the same presence if it were hanging off the side of a table. Occasionally, you'll see a flag that is lowered on the staff. This is called half-mast. This is done when the nation or a state observes the death of someone, but the lowered flag doesn't fly alone. The top position that it previously held is now occupied by the invisible death flag, and so the flag we know and see all the time yields to death, for a time.

As an aside, the flag is considered a living thing and I don't think it should be desecrated. *Disclaimer*: This writer is a veteran of the U.S. Army. You might see an upside-down national flag on an ambulance as this means there is a state of emergency – a life or death situation, but you never see an upside-down flag on a police vehicle. Isn't that something? The United States will yield to death in a life or death situation, but her system of laws and order will not. That's leadership!

I define leadership as a discipline for the leader. Now, let's apply this example to an individual leader, and let's replace the word flag with standard which is another word for flag. We can keep the word staff as it can also mean a group of people. This kind of staff is holding you, the leader, up with the work that they do. It's your job as the standard to hold your position. To lower the standard would mean that some other standard flies above you and, by default, above your staff. We should not relax or lower our standard. To do this would leave us alone, to restore it to its proper place.

Being a leader is like being a flag. You will seemingly stand alone and weather storms. Not too many people will give thought to either, but we expect them to be there no matter what.

Politicians rally people around their cause and military commanders rally their troops around them. This is the weaponization of leadership. You see the difference? Both are effective methods as they draw out the emotions of those that follow them.

People respond better if they are rallied around a leader instead of by a goal set for them.

I think this is difficult for some leaders to understand. They insist that sharing the goal, and the progress to the goal, alone will motivate their teams. There is no emotion in a number, and so the goal won't be met if the emotions of the people are not met.

We've explored a lot about ego, relationships, leadership, and ourselves which is in us. Let's look at how we break leadership down for our people.

Gentle Reminder: Run for a coach, run to a mentor.

Applied Leadership

Applied Leadership is the practice of mentoring and coaching others to construct your vision.

C oaching is the preparation and mentoring the execution of your vision. Additionally, you sell your vision to others. You don't give it to them. *Applied Leadership* without the benefit of relationship to those you lead is bullying. The same can be said for relationships without the benefit of leadership.

Think of *Applied Leadership* as rearing a child. At first, you coach them by communicating to their emotions. You want them to feel good. You meet them where they are, literally on the ground floor, which is the foundation of their lives. Always smiling and encouraging them, and then as they grow older and you expect them to do age-appropriate things, you mentor them with challenges, you speak to their intellect. You're leading them into becoming a well-adjusted adult.

Let's look at the other side of this equation. From the child's point of view, you can do no wrong. You were always there to make corrections, fix things, chastise, and wipe tears. This is until the child came of age and realized that parents make mistakes too. Parents are not perfect. Some of them divorce, miscalculate their finances, or lose the ability to hide their own shortcomings. The home was a microcosm of the world. And then, the child needed others to coach and mentor them. It's the cycle of life.

Remember your first big purchase? There was effort, and then reward, and then responsibly. It seemed like we were stuck with the effects of the latter longer than the benefits of the former. In all the years I led people and asked them what a leader is, no one ever said, "Someone who makes difficult decisions that affect the lives of others." The responsibility you felt after making that first major purchase is primordial leadership.

It sets the stage for how we react or respond to responsibility.

The advantage of *Applied Leadership* in work production gives the appearance of arching a timeline so that the end point is the same, but you appear to get more done. You will gain the hearts and minds of people. You will get them to do more than you ask of them.

Applied Leadership as a practice is broken down into two areas they are: **coaching and mentoring.**

Coaching is the beginning of the work. Leaders could spend most of their time in this practice area, or at least they should. This is where relationships are made with staff. This is where they get to see you as one of them, which is important because when you switch to mentoring, they may feel differently about you.

Mentoring is the means by which you test, perfect, and teach the mentee. You would be wise to study both areas. They are not epaulettes, but the form and function of the responsibility of leadership. The epaulettes are the character of the leader that must be developed and maintained.

Coaching is a critical first step to leading others, as it will help you get to know them. Now, the best coaching in the world doesn't guarantee a successful outcome.

Applied Leadership: Direct

This is *Applied Leadership* directed to an individual in the shortest possible span of time in order to achieve a desperate end.

I recall an interview I went to where the interviewer shared some critical dates for the new hire to be a part of – that's all I need to hear. I repeated the dates two more times during interview. One of those times I assured the interviewer that I could make myself available to start in time for the important dates.

Yes, I led the interview to an employment decision that was in my favor. In the *Thank You* letter I emailed to the interviewer, I once again made mention of the dates and my availability. At the end of the interview I tried to close the deal by asking, "Can we close this deal today?" Now, I was told that there would be another interview and the decision would be made at that time, but at least I got the second interview.

Note: If you're not leading the employers to make hiring decisions in your favor, you're just being interrogated at your interviews. An interrogation not good – it's just a series of questions and answers which can only end in one of two next steps.

One: nothing, which would be good as you get to go home.

Two: they read you your rights and you had to stay for a while.

Now, in an interview for employment, the latter would never happen, but the former is an experience that many job seekers will have, and that is nothing – no call back and no job, but at least they get to home after the interview.

One thing is for sure though – it's highly unlikely that someone who has been interrogated would have answered the questions so well that the police offered them a job.

We Like Our Shortcuts

Gentle Reminder: Life hacks are dangerous life shortcuts.

There are four types of coaching:

- Coaching for well-being
- Coaching for ego
- Cross coaching
- Coaching for Performance

I've heard people say they need a mentor. And I've heard other people who overheard that statement say, "What you need is a swift kick in your butt." Neither is necessary for the person that has shortcomings as we can all stand to improve in some area(s). Mentoring alone will not always work as the person needs discipline to be mentored and your methods of mentoring should be built upon coaching, as that is where the beginning of the relationship is. The person in question doesn't need to be a superstar to be mentored, but they must show discipline and a have a constitution that can take up the challenge.

Some parents understand this by way of experience. They know that there are times when they parent their children, times when they mentor their children, and times when they coach their children. They may not define it as such, but it is the same nonetheless.

My son's soccer coach is a good example of this. He does not show his own children, who are on the team, favoritism – good for him. He will issue swift correction when shortcomings are present to all his players, but he will also show tenderness when a child is hurt physically or emotionally. In fact, it's quite amusing to see him and his daughter shouting at each other across the field. Seeing them in those very raw moments keeps me quiet when my son gets his rebuke from the coach.

And, you know what? Expression, communication, understanding disappointment, and even anger are as much a part of the game as scoring or winning. The coach's communication is clear, and we all understand what he means and what he wants. While his title is that of coach, the example I cited above has him wearing both the coaching and mentoring hats.

Coaching Corporately

Energy can't be destroyed, but you can run out of it. Is the team tired? When we make plans, they usually have the team as the dominator and the workload as the numerator. We believe all things are equal, and so we do the math and expect the number we need because the equation is solid, but the state of the team is the real denominator.

Some companies mistakenly think that the right leadership will make people happy – this is not true. Not even *Applied Leadership* will make people happy. Don't get me wrong, personality makes difficult situations bearable, some leaders can put us in a good humor, but that doesn't last long, and that's not happy.

If you say your job is not to make your staff happy, you're wrong. Your company is responsible for the quality of life of your workers. If this was your belief, "Just get the work done," and you're not concerned with quality of life, they are talking about you.

What is it called when you kill a people's culture? There's a word for it. It's called ethnocide. By suppressing the culture of your company, you're killing it. This form of suppression is conscious. If you are not trying to do this, but achieve the same result, you may be repressing the culture of your company. I'll call this officide. It's the decay of the company culture. You know I have an example of this, right?

Prior to the job I have now, I went to an interview for a company that had an owner that believed abusing candidates was the most efficient form of venting. Now, at first, I thought this was just his disposition, but I soon came to realize that this was also his leadership style. He said unflattering things about his staff, he shared the personal business of people that we mutually knew, and he told me point blank that he didn't care for my opinions. His rationale is flawed as he only created resentment in me, and possibly fear in his employees. Now, I really needed the job and I think I could have endured him for a while, but what would I have gained?

Gangs understand this. They offer their prospects security, money, respect, power, family, a new name, exclusivity, and freedom. They even refer to the gang as a nation. They will have bi-laws, rules, enforcement, and witness intimidation. This is their culture. I'm sure fear of leaving the gang will keep them together, but it's not what brought them together.

Once everyone understands the culture, they support it. I would argue that the number of orders and assignments given are disproportionally low in comparison to its breadth as the members will not only follow their leaders, but they will also follow the organization's culture. Its leaders sell the culture and the culture knits. Even people who are not a part of the gang are a part of the culture. You've heard it said that snitches get stitches. *Gansta Rap* was a dominant force in music of the 90's – that's a culture.

Establish a strong company culture and retain more talent. Sell that same awesome culture and attract better-qualified talent. Sell the company and you get workers – hit or miss proposition, as some people just want a job. Sell the culture and get a movement. Now, that will extend beyond your company walls. People want to belong to something. And, if they feel like they belong they will support. It's not so hard to see. In fact, it's plain to see, there is a better way.

Why hold a light up to the veil when you can just move it?

Coaching for Well-Being

This is clearly for quality of life. Your benefit to delivering this kind of coaching is indirect as your focus is the well being of the individual.

If you're both coach and mentor to this person you would have to be skillful. You can't bounce back and forth from one practice area to the other. When you coach someone in the *Applied Leadership* model, you enter a *Coaching Circumference*. At first, it may be small as the person is closed off and emotions surround their ego, at the epicenter. The outer most layer is the primary wall and this is where you initially contacted them - you asked to talk. The secondary layer is harder to get to because you need to get through all the things they need to talk about. There is venting of details, a sense of injustice, and a host of other case-specific things.

Logic doesn't work here, but you knew that already. You want them to feel good about talking, moving to resolve, healing, and exploring next steps.

Inside of the *Coaching Circumference* (CC), will consist of you, the coach, and the staff member. To add or invite more coaches would make the endeavor look like an intervention which could have undesirable effects on the person being coached.

Things Happen: Coaching Circumference

Sometimes people clash or make grievous errors in judgment.

If you're coaching someone after an incident, the further away you start from the epicenter (person being coached), the more effective your coaching program will be.

Conversely, the closer you start your coaching program to someone before an incident can occur the more responsive, they will be to the coaching you were providing.

Providing the coaching was presented to them on a set schedule. If you wait until after an incident, believing this is more cost effective, you may lose more in the end with a difficult situation than had you employed a coaching program to begin with. These programs are nothing more than dialogue about how they feel in certain situations and how they typically respond.

We're coaching feelings even when the task at hand is to coach for a specific task. If someone is not performing well, they may feel a certain way about it. I'm saying we need to take the time to find out. It may not take long to find out. It is possible to coach a group of people.

Example: your team feels a certain way about something. You can speak to their feelings in a group setting, but mentoring is a privilege reserved for you to do one-on-one.

Still, be prepared to coach some, if not all, of them individually – it's case by case.

Coaching for Ego

Just as it sounds this form of coaching goes right to the core of a person. There are some undesirable traits that the person possesses. Remember, the key here is to be positive, supportive, and encouraging.

If you're coaching a subordinate leader, you may be saving countless careers by doing this. If you're coaching a staff member, possibly a future leader, you're better preparing them for work. And, because coaching principles are universal, you may be better preparing them for home as well.

No doubt about it, coaching is the hardest part of your job. It's thankless because when done correctly, they will think it's about the relationship not them.

Coaching for Performance

It's not that people set out to have poor performance. It's that they arrive there.

Paper tiger eats a paper lamb.

I've covered corrective action a few times. This is a tough part of a leader's job. I think the term corrective action is. It's a situation on a piece of paper. Earlier, I said a situation is something we have power to change, while a condition is something, we have lesser power to change. The situation outlined in a corrective action seems like a condition to the recipient, as there are conditions to be met.

Call me a softy, but I hate corrective actions. The paper that the corrective action is written on cannot change someone. Paper doesn't change people. If you received a college degree today, this didn't change you. The change you made took place during the run-up to the degree being awarded to you.

If you were married today, the marriage certificate didn't change you. Sure, your marital status changed, but it did not change you. You changed during the courtship and engagement to become someone that someone else saw as marriage material.

Last example, a child will be born prior to the birth certificate being issued. The certificate didn't change the child. And so, the corrective action in and of itself will never change someone. The change comes from the leader that presents it.

You'll have to lead the team member out of this situation. This is perhaps one of the most powerful examples of leadership. Don't put the paper before you, as it will not lead the person out of the corrective action. Remember, it's their emotions we want to coach, and we want them to see the changes that are needed, and we want them to suggest the way they go about bringing the change.

This is the preferred method as the more you do for someone the more they will expect you to do for them. So, you're not trying to get them out of poor performance, you want to lead them out. We can't leave performance to chance. We need an effective coaching program in place. We have to train people, coach people, and mentor people.

Some managers will train their team, and then charge them to produce something that can be quantified. If you don't coach people through what you outline as success, how will each team member achieve the same result? They will all feel differently about the work, you, the goal, each other, the day of the week, etc.

We need to understand what they feel and what they think. We need to set the tone and periodically reset the tone. Let me offer this, you may have had a meeting with your team to inquire about their performance. They might have told you that they feel some kind of way about how some other department is doing or not doing.

Do you see that? They're tying performance into feelings, based on some external factor. This part could be familiar too. If you asked how long they've been feeling this way, they might respond for three months. You may choose not to believe, but you could have known had you been coaching them. You may not be able to change all the external factors, but you can change how they perceive them which will determine how hey feel about them.

Without a system of reward, you cannot have only a system of punishment - that's draconian.

Cross Coaching

The only form of coaching that is malignant to the well being of someone being coached.

In the earliest form of cross coaching, we saw Eve being cross-coached by the serpent. His coaching wasn't for her benefit, as it was for his. He let pride get the best of him. This coach, led by his ego, cross coached the first family.

Here, we see that there is a one to one ratio of leader to coach, but today, there are more than a thousand coaches per leader. Many of the people you lead will coach others. If their coaching is intended to coach to your vision, it's fine. However, some coaches engage in *Cross Coaching*.

This is where their efforts counter your purpose. It's not so easy because cross coaching is directed at ego via your emotions. The serpent is the father of cross coaching. He tempted Eve to do something to get something he himself did not do. Since we know that coaches are plentiful, we need to have a solid coaching plan in place for the team. Don't wait for difficult times to do this.

Now, without a coaching plan in place, how would the plethora of coaches motivate others or themselves? Since coaching is a tool used to address emotions, and since emotions are at the root of most workplace issues, you could have the makings of a perfect storm.

Coaches are popular. People want to talk to them and dress like them. They will even wait in line just to engage in random conversation because the coach makes them feel good.

The mentor has an air of confidence and ease with them. This is the person that comes around and you know everything will be all right. This is because the mentor has been there before. They have become selective with who they mentor. They speak matter-of-factly and listen with their ears, eyes, and thoughts.

Now, I said applied leadership is both coaching and mentoring. If you're a coach and you want to mentor, you'll have to get closer to the archetype that I outlined. This is when you will make leaps of faith for yourself. Someone should have mentored you.

We don't lead people. We lead relationships with people – through the coaching of their emotions, and by mentoring their intellect.

Things to remember when coaching:

Don't make yourself bigger than the situation - this is the mentor's role. You're taking away from their time. Counselors know that they should never tell their client that they have an issue. I'm saying take the step of finding out why they feel the way they do.

So, you're thinking I want you to be a counselor or a therapist? No, when we were infants we lived in a world of emotions and feelings. We communicated this way until we could verbalize. Now that we're grown up, our communication has a duality. It is verbal and emotional.

We experience emotion first, and then we express feelings. Some of us are particularly adept at hiding our feelings, but our emotions reside under the surface. So, focus on the feelings that you perceive the person expressing. This will take practice as we could get this wrong. The best way to start is by asking, "How do you feel about this?"

When someone is telling you how they are feeling never cut them off. If they repeat themselves you can repeat what they say, to let them know you have heard them.

Mentoring

Relationship Application – I must firmly prepare my relationships with people with load-bearing discussions before I load them with the expectations of mentoring.

When providing feedback from the mentor mindset, we're focused on the person's thought process. How will they approach the project or task in the future, based on what we just learned? Here, we are the subject matter expert, but we're trying to make them one too, and so we need to coax them into offering solutions.

Now, if a supervisor finds that they are mentoring more than one staff at a time, this can be taxing for them and eventually affect their performance and quality of life. We can wait for their monthly supervision to ask them or encourage them not to wait that long but to disclose this in real-time.

You'd be surprised how quickly mentoring others can sneak up on you. This is especially true if you are new to leadership and have a zeal to improve everything. Just because you had success before doesn't guarantee you'll have success now. So, it's not just the complexities involved with mentoring, it's also the volume of mentees at any given time.

In my career, I interviewed for two promotions that I didn't get. I thought I was ready, but maybe I wasn't. I didn't have a mentor at those times. And, I didn't reach out to anyone to talk about it. I've now learned that I should stay in practice for leadership and stay close to people who are where I want to be.

Active mentoring is when someone takes us under their wing for development.

Passive mentoring is when we identify someone we can model ourselves after. This is someone that will let us stay close due to proximity of work or mutual interests. They may not deliberately share with us, but we benefit from being an associate.

I also had a lot of experience at the time I went for those interviews. Maybe my pride got in the way of reaching out for guidance. And so, we'll need the Epaulette's not only for leadership, but also to receive coaching and mentoring from others.

What about promotions?

The itch for promotion is a cell phone case of a different color. An itch is an irritant, not motivation, or providence. That itch is sell serving – don't buy into it! A mentor will tell you if promotion is a good idea for you, but a coach will prepare you just because you said you want a promotion.

So, if you have no mentor to discuss promotion, you're on your own. Few people are humble enough to seek out a mentor once they attain a higher position. The excitement and accomplishment can blindside them. Smart people ask lots of questions and they point their career compass in the direction of someone that is where they want to be.

The coach conditions you entirely based on what you already know. The focus is how you feel about your ability, and how your ability fits with the machine that is the team.

The mentor will prepare you for what you don't think you can do. If it is evident to them, the mentor will declare that you are ready for the next level and it is time to do just that.

I can't mentor you from where you started. I can only coach you from there. You'll have to come to me.

If you're the kind of leader that raises your voice at your team when you're angry, then you are more closely aligned with your principles. You have left your purpose because your purpose is not to scold people.

Correction is done correctly when you can subtly mask your intellect with a coach's emotions, which are encouraging. And yes, you want to connect with their emotions, but if you are noticeably angry, you will surface their reactive emotions – which could be to lay blame, deflect, point out flaws in the plan, etc.

You want them to respond to you, but not negatively. We should use the sandwich technique where you say something encouraging, then go for the best of the problem, and finally end on an upswing. Talking angry to people is like digging a hole in the relationship landscape. And, just because you stopped talking angry doesn't mean you filled the hole in. It will just sit there and repeating this shortcoming will only dig the hole deeper.

Workplace Culture

Without leadership and an internal purpose-driven culture, it will be difficult to retain talent. Now, if staff shortages appear, you will have effectively tied your first line of supervisors' hands. They will be forced to forego staff shortcomings for fear of driving away the remaining staff. If the initial issue was based on poor morale, doing more of the same thing won't reverse this trend.

The strength of your team is in its diversity. It's a beautiful thing when we become indifferent to our differences. And, if they can work together to achieve a corporate goal that is awesome. This is successfully done each day somewhere.

Now, how can we reproduce this in our respective shops? Well, if culture is something we identify with, something we find strength in, something we desire to preserve, something we may even fight for, then we can reproduce this at the office. Some companies have learned this as they have been named best place to work for.

Be the leader that puts workplace culture before profits.

Workers will see that and give more of themselves and culture doesn't require that you be a leader of a specific tribe to influence society.

What is Workplace Culture?

A big part of workplace culture is socialization. Yes, workers like to talk, congregate, sometimes do non-work-related things, but more importantly the workplace is an extension of our personal lives. We always say we spend more time at work than at home. At work, some people fall in love with each other, some fall out with each other, they may eat lunch together, or make plans to meet up after work.

That's a lot of stuff that doesn't make it to your bottom line. Now, if I asked you what kind of workplace culture you have, you might have to pause to think about it, right? What if I asked how you, as a leader, contribute to workplace culture? I'm sure if you think long enough you can come up something, but your effort may not have been intentional.

It could be that you are personable and witty – that's nice, but:

- What is different or special about your team?
- What conscious steps do you take towards the quality of life for your team?
- Do you leave fun up to the team?
- Are you too busy to join in and participate?
- Are you too serious and professional to participate?

That last line should be read with a low gruff voice. Workplace culture is not like quality of life initiatives because the latter needs to be approved by upper management, but culture is what you make it, or what you allow you team to make.

Workplace culture includes your values. What you need to make happen consistently, and what you will not allow. Some supervisors buy snacks, which is always nice.

Tell me about the work environment:

- Is it a friendly place to work?
- Does all the technology function properly?
- How long does it take to receive supply?
- Aside from pay and an overhaul for computer systems, are there office issues that remain after multiple complaints?
- Is there a system in place to address and provide updates for complaints?
- Do you have a system of rewards?

New hires will follow the supervisor for a few days to a few weeks, but then something happens. They start to follow relationships. People are more inclined to follow relationships than leaders. They'll gravitate to people they identify with. Those relationships usually point the now new hire to the culture of the company. Statements surface like, "Well, here we do things like this!"

Since you can't lead the new hire every minute of every day you need to leave them in a culture that will support your leadership. If not, you're playing the lottery with your performance.

Culture is powerful in that once a culture is established, you can't go back – you can't un-culture. New leadership can come in, but if they add all that new leadership stuff to the same old culture it could wash out.

It will take a talented individual to uncover the culture, determine its use, steer the team away from it, and produce a new culture to replace what the people will believe they've lost. And, still do your meetings, payroll, monthly metrics, and everything else. What helps most with culture, other than developing or shaping it, is coaching your team one-on-one. We know they will behave differently in a coaching setting.

I Doubt It

Everyone faces doubt at some point. We'll doubt our ability, doubt out course of action, and probability of success. This is normal, but I want you to understand that ego has a place in this situation. If you vetted, planned, trained, prepared, and led via Applied Leadership, your team to the vision you have, you should receive a measure of success.

Now, if after all this is in place you still have doubt, that's probably fear. An amount of fear is okay as it will force us to proceed with caution, however, fear can be a product of a weekend ego. If your fear is that you can't do it, how you will look upon failing, or what you stand to lose, then you are betraying your vision and all the supports that it has. At the time you commit to your vision with all that it needs to launch, it's no longer about you. This is very hard to come to terms with as we see with so many entrepreneurs.

They run their vision like it itself is a business. You can't run a vision. You lead people to it. Protect your vision from yourself and keep the integrity of it for the sake of those you lead. Write down the vision in as much detail as you can.

Make a *Vision Statement*, which consists of:

- Purpose
- Premise
- Benefit

Brace for Impact

Some believe North Korean leaders do this by speaking to the emotion of fear in their people. Cult leaders will keep their followers in a perpetual state of emotion by promising or reinforcing the feelings of salvation, and of course, the leader or party is the solution.

Hitler did this by holding rallies to stir up and impart his feelings to his people. The idea is to charge the people and incite them to act on or maintain your agenda. North Korea taking on the US without nuclear weapons is like someone taking curse words to a gunfight – that's not going to work. That's like their best Sunday suit. Even if it's bursting at the seams, it's still their best Sunday suit.

And, what's the impact of this? Complete dominance of a people. Now, North Korea perceives US policy as bullying. So, what does the US do? They release information about the North Korean leader's mental state and the poverty his people live in. And, despite all this, there is no public outcry about it. It's not that Americans don't care, but how can America have a nuclear arsenal and tell another sovereign nation that they can't have one too?

What's next? Ban people we deem as mental from reproducing or holding public office? It's a rhetorical question, but by what standard would we judge someone's mentally fitness to wield nuclear weapons?

Bottom line: If you feel like you're being bullied, you will want what the bully has so you can defend yourself.

Say It Don't Spray It

Diplomacy, like leadership can be broken down into coaching and mentoring. That is on a micro level. Now, on a macro level, involving nations, it's usually gunboat diplomacy. This is using military strength to shape your foreign policy and ultimately deliver your diplomatic exchange. Of course, we understand dollar diplomacy shares meeting time too as choking off trade usually gets desirable results. But that's not working against North Korea.

Call me naïve, but I don't think it's a good idea to demonize a nation and then ask them to make concessions. Coach and then mentor the leader.

Negotiating

The longer you wait the weaker your position is.

Yes, you guessed it! Negotiating can be broken down into coaching and mentoring, just like leadership and diplomacy. Start with the end in mind. Coach the person into feeling good about closing the deal. Talk to them about what they stand to gain. Don't bother telling them what you stand to lose or give up.

Never negotiate who stands to lose the most. By disclosing what you stand to lose you hold them in the negotiating pattern, because now they think you two are negotiating about what you're giving up instead of what you get. Start by asking, "So, what brings you to the negotiation today?" Ask them, "How do you feel about walking out of here with what you want?"

Our line of questioning should be subtle. They shouldn't be able to discern if our questions are well-placed curiosity, or just courtesy. My negotiations wouldn't be predicated on dollar amount alone. I often tell my opponent that I'm only going to do two rounds with them, take it, or leave it.

This is an interesting dynamic that puts pressure on them, but it also prepares them to be mentored. Now, they know they get two chances to make a deal. If they're willing to go more than that, they can keep it/have it.

This disposition will work wonders for you before the negotiations even begin because they perceived you as already winning the preliminary round and now, they only have three chances to persuade you.

And, of course, relationships can be broken into coaching and mentoring. The principles are the same as the others. The major difference is that personal relationships carry more emotions with them, and we more readily express them too.

Finally, we can coach people into relationships.

You know, you can coach people. Look, I like this conversation. Here's my number – you can call me anytime. If I don't answer I might be in the shower, you know, because I take showers every day. Or, I might be eating or something. I might answer after a few rings, but no more than four because my voicemail will pick up. Okay, call me!

Great talking to you! You made some good points, although, I disagree with one of them. Look, we ran out of time, I need to go. We had a nice talk I'd like to get your thoughts on some other topics – give me a call.

Okay, let's debrief, the first person doesn't get a callback. This is an example of a lonely heart. They talked too much and offered a lot of circumstantial information. It's as if they were having both parts of the conversation.

I believe this person goes home at night, sits in a chair and waits for tomorrow to come. Not that this is a bad person, but they're not coaching, they're begging. The call to action at the end didn't connect to the begging before it.

Now, the second example is straightforward. The thing to do is to get the person you're coaching to feel good. If you made the person feel good, they will call you, because they want to feel good again.

What's Your Nomenclature?

Gentle Reminder: It's not what you call yourself – it's how you define yourself.

I had a director that had us do a great exercise. She had each of us pass around a piece of paper with our name on it. Each person on the team had to write down one word on that sheet that represented the person whose name was on it. We passed the sheets around a few times until each paper with our names on it contained those words that described us. Everyone, including me, seemed pleased with the words to describe them.

Now, I was only on the team for six weeks and I only worked with two of them daily as we were scattered across multiple locations, but they were spot on for me. So, my personal brand didn't need to be a visual one. My emails, phone calls, the work hat I did preceded me.

It's a great exercise that all teams should try.

So, I didn't have to tell people what I am or what I represent, I carried myself the way I define myself and they saw this too. I am a strong believer in looking like your future. You'll see that's a chapter in this book as well.

What are people saying about you?

And, what do you want people to say about you? Before you answer those questions, I have another: Where are you right now?

No, I don't mean physically, I mean categorically. We arrived at this place today because of where we were yesterday. Today's thoughts need to line up with the vision we have of tomorrow. That being said, let's explore the topic of *Nomenclature*.

Gentle Reminder: The future was paid for today and everyday pays for the future.

 Let's reverse this to read: Where you want to be tomorrow should determine where you are today.

Relatively Relative

Nomenclature is a term used to describe something. This will help someone understand exactly what you are referring to. A popular form of nomenclature would be of a scientific nature.

Example: The term homo sapiens refers to human beings. That's fine in a scientific sense, but what about in the workplace or in a personal relationship. We would need more than just a human being. What are the person's characteristics, capabilities, strengths, weaknesses, etc.?

Nomenclature is not a definition of something as a definition is finite, with a period at the end.

Example: in the US Army an infantryman is an 11B. This doesn't tell us anything more than what the person does for a living. We don't have any specific information about the individual infantryman.

Are we defining ourselves or describing ourselves? What's the first word you would use to describe yourself? Don't use static words that are empty but sound nice. We need to incorporate verbs because our description should have us doing something.

It's the doing that gets us to the goal.

Defining others is understandable because we have a natural tendency to define people in order to determine if they are a threat or asset to us. People will do this to us as well. There is a danger if we fail to develop a nomenclature for ourselves, and the people within our sphere of influence. Someone else could come along, and the usually do, to assign a nomenclature that, by design, is advantageous to them.

Let's start with our children. Without assigning them starter nomenclature that is derived from the one we developed for our family, children can be open game for unsavory associations.

Take gangs for instance. They have elaborate handshakes, colors and symbolism that represent the nomenclature of who they are. Often a name is given to new members based on something they are known for. Let's assume that the gang thinks the recruit is crazy. That recruit would now feel compelled to live up to the moniker given to them, in addition to the values that are instilled from the gang.

The more you accept what you are called the more likely you are to fulfill it – this is self-perpetuating. Additionally, many gangs have a charter, or some set of strict rules to observe. Failure to adhere to these rules can have dire consequences. And so, you see there are multiple mechanisms in place to maintain the integrity of the gang culture via the influence of the gang's corporate nomenclature.

Okay, you're not in a gang, but you lead a team of workers. I think a good leader that takes over a new team will first get to know everyone, share their vision of what the future looks like, and ask how they can best support each person's position. But a fatal mistake would be to fail to assign a nomenclature to the team.

This is in line with the company culture which we'll cover a little later. Of course, you'll get their input which would be used, added to your supervisor's vision and expectations.

All you do in those first weeks and months should address this. And, you must reinforce this periodically, or someone else on the team will do this for you. While the person or persons that do this may not be bad people, they would lean the team towards their understanding and benefit. After all, a major dynamic changed the team from the top (you), and you need to pull everyone together.

What about our children? They will all face a bully, or bless their little hearts, they may engage in bullying behavior. There is a belief that people who bully others have insecurities. Similarly, people who are more susceptible to bullies may have insecurities.

What if we helped our children to develop a nomenclature that tells them who they are? They can have confidence in that and themselves. We can tell them, "Who you are equates to value, purpose, expectation, acceptance, gratitude, fortitude, and love of self."

This would leave little room in that child's life to look for these things in others or to crush it if they see it in others.

Flash forward twenty years in the life of that child. They're looking for love. If they developed nomenclature, they would look for someone that would complement their own. This is a best fit. If they don't have personal nomenclature they would search on a very superficial level.

Without knowing oneself a person can be empty. Leave that the person empty long enough and just about anyone can fill the emptiness. But the emptiness is a lack of self. No one can truly fill that void. Imagine, trying to find someone that possesses characteristics that we ourselves do not possess.

Are we taking a similar approach to how we describe ourselves?

Why do you need to know your nomenclature? Well, how you perceive yourself has a direct correlation to how successful you will be. And, this may also have an impact on how others perceive you as well.

Establishing your nomenclature is important, as this will help us to fend off others from imprinting or projecting on you. Keeping yourself clear and free of outside negative influences will help to protect your vision and those you lead or serve.

Coaching with Nomenclature

Don't look for opportunities – find them!

This is a mindset. To say you are looking for something is a start, but to say that you will find something is a goal met! The proper phrasing will nicely support your nomenclature statement about yourself.

If you are a nice person you don't have to say this. You would simply share something you've done and the person you are speaking with would come to that conclusion.

Beware of the person that leads you to believe what and who they are. Often, people do this to mislead us. Recall the last time someone sold you something that turned out to undesirable. Part of the reason you made that purchase was because they led you to trust them, right? Or, they spent more time selling themselves than the product out service. The salesperson was, not only good at defining their nomenclature, but also good at discerning you. Apparently better than you were.

Don't feel bad, when you went in to make the purchase you didn't remember your nomenclature. We only do this instinctively, and I want you to do this consistently. That's the only difference between you and that salesperson.

Your name is more than a name given to you, you are given to it – what will you do to maintain it?

You want nomenclature to be in the active tense. You are initiating the event. The inverse of this is the passive tense, and here the event is happening to you.

I describe myself as an advocate for the well being of others.

If you believe leadership is close to you, you should embrace it because it should be a part of you. If you think you're close to it, you'll have to work for it. No, I'm not splitting hairs – it's not the same thing.

Leadership is you the leader. It's the outward and inward expression of your ability to lead. If you know how difficult it is to lead others you wouldn't run to this type of responsibility. People have high expectations of their leaders, and your expectation of yourself would likely be higher than theirs.

Okay, you're a leader, you have a purpose, you have a vision, but what do you look like today, in relation to your vision?

Look Like Your Future

Your vision is a place, a time, and a mindset!

I've told many aspiring leaders and newly promoted ones that you must look like your future.

Dreamers have vision. They have a picture of what the future will be. A leader will act upon that vision of the future today, right now. You may have heard the expression: The future starts today! You want to look like your future, right now.

The future is only possible once we begin working on it. If we delay the start, then the future will eventually become the present. As we look back to this day, it will be the past. Today, is already the past in the future you started working for. From that point in the future, what did you do today?

I developed this thought while working with job seekers. I had a group that was as diverse as the general population. At times I found it difficult to get my point across to the entire group. I thought it was interesting that the most vocal, and sometimes most disruptive, job seekers were also the most adamant about what they wanted in the future.

To my surprise, they had wanted to work in the social services field. In fact, we discussed ways in which we could discipline our children, yet these adults, these parents, that are participating in my class, could benefit from discipline themselves. I wondered, what kind of social worker would cut off others to speak and say immature things? What kind of social worker must be pulled to the side and be rebuked for their behavior?

It was then that I thought to tell them, and countless others, that we need to look like our future. Whatever that person is that you will be a few years from now needs to be evident in you right now.

We need to look like our future. The longer we wait to do this, the longer we will look like our present. Imagine, the disappointment of arriving at what should look like in the future, only to see what you already have.

No, this is not about fashion or appearance. It's how you engage the future. It's a practice that brings discipline to you right now and discipline to the way you view the future. You know you stand out and it doesn't matter.

There is a level of discomfort with looking like the future while in the present. People may not understand you. You're doing twice the work and you're practicing.

After practice, some things that would bother people right now don't seem to have the same gravity for you. I want to be clear though, looking like the future is not living in the future. You can be fully engaged with today, but we're conscious of how the engagement will fit into our future. There's a balance that must be observed or you stand to lose.

It's like investment options. You know, there are long-term, low risk investments, and high-risk short-term investments. I refuse to be another Smith. An agent of complacency and an ideal assimilation of protected norms. I conduct myself like an executive, but I work like payday is tomorrow. I hold an expectation and hunger for my pay. If I want to eat every day, I must work every day.

Gentle Reminder References

1. Gentle Reminder: Leaders coach emotions and mentor intellect.
2. Gentle Reminder: Start your day with the end of the day in mind.
3. Gentle Reminder: The best way to be humble is to be grateful.
4. Gentle Reminder: Successful leaders impart emotion to their teams and impart their intellect.
5. Gentle Reminder: The future was paid for today and everyday pays for the future.
6. Gentle Reminder: If you think you're *The GOAT*, you'll have to feed the goat!
7. Gentle Reminder: Leaders are born in and raised out of trouble.
8. Gentle Reminder: We run for coaches, but we run to mentors.
9. Gentle Reminder: When Opportunity comes, I want it to see me as opportunity!

10. Gentle Reminder: Make it easy for people to work with you and they will want to work for you.

11. Gentle Reminder: Lead your purpose, manage your principles.

12. Gentle Reminder: Don't nest in your situation.

13. Gentle Reminder: Growth is a product of growth.

14. Gentle Reminder: Winner's don't make the trophy, they take it.

15. Gentle Reminder: Company culture is a perishable asset.

16. Gentle Reminder: Leadership is not control.

17. Gentle Reminder: Make moments not time.

18. Gentle Reminder: Once mentored you become a mentor.

19. Gentle Reminder: Life hacks are dangerous life shortcuts.

20. Gentle Reminder: Growth = change.

21. Gentle Reminder: Anything that doesn't profit you will cost you.

22. Gentle Reminder: What you do in a situation will determine how you get out of a situation.

23. Gentle Reminder: You lead people to your vision, or you lead them to your ego.

24. Gentle Reminder: Leadership is not about self, it's about vision.

25. Gentle Reminder: Leadership is a discipline for you, not the people you serve!

26. Gentle Reminder: Relationships are about communication and action.

27. Gentle Reminder: People give you the perspective of leadership and you give them the perspective of vision.

28. Gentle Reminder: The beginning of your trouble is the beginning of your training.

29. Gentle Reminder: Love work, work love.

30. Gentle Reminder: It's not what you call yourself, it's how you define yourself.

31. Gentle Reminder: You can't have success and comfort at the same time.

32. Gentle Reminder: Small insignificant opportunities prepare use for big opportunities.

The Seven Epaulettes of Leadership

The Epaulettes of Leadership are key character traits the leaders must possess for themselves and for those they lead.

T here is something attractive about great leadership and something intriguing about poor leadership. We spend a lot of time analyzing poor leaders to discern or determine why this is the case, but we seldom analyze great leaders in the same way.

I identified them when I reviewed why I thought some people were good leaders. I also looked at my own career and identified moments when I was most effective.

I once worked for a company where a senior leader would always say "Leaders lead!" This was the charge that was given - it meant, "Leaders get out there and lead."

The charge was usually given to us in the face of some difficult situations, but what does that mean? Does it mean go forth, go first, talk tough, motivate people, or all the above? If we don't define and teach leadership for subordinates, how can we call for it? You could get subordinate leaders working from habit or experience which may not be advantageous to the team.

I once had a staff member that struggled to get to work on time, was at odds with the team and clients, would not respond to my coaching, and was able to secure a job as a supervisor in another company. This person argued every point, even when they knew they were wrong, even when there was no reason to argue. This person even told me that they would enjoy more success than I did.

Maybe, in some bizarro world where everything is backwards he would be a great manager, and I would be a terrible worker. I would be reprimanded for coming to work on time and completing my work. He would yell at me for working hard and say, "This is bizarro world, where everything is backwards, and don't you get it? I'd like to punish you for your good deeds, but instead I must reward you, because, this is bizarro world and everything is backwards here!"

So, we talked about the new role on his last day of employment with us. I'm not sure why I was surprised that he didn't want any advice from me. I had wanted to share how I split up my day and some pitfalls I made when I first started out. He would hear none of it. He was gloating in his success and quite proud of himself. I wished him well and I still do. I think he meant well. I just couldn't get close enough to uncover the root of his actions and words. There was no rhyme of reason to it.

I later learned that things didn't work out so well for him. I wasn't happy about that either – I counted him as one of mine. There is a Native American saying that comes to mind: You can't wake someone that is pretending to be asleep.

This man clearly possessed some of the epaulettes, but his ego would get the best of him. Sure, you can still lead people, but I said earlier, you'll either lead people to your vision or lead them to your ego.

Gentle Reminder: The beginning of your trouble is the beginning of your training.

Imagine, being installed to a position of authority, not being properly equipped, not being taught to succeed, and not realizing that your design is to fail. During this same time, I had a colleague who faced a staff shortage, he had a difficult boss, his metrics were poor, and he couldn't find quality candidates.

These situations helped to spur me on to take notes for what would become my first book. Back to my colleague, after he shared his situation, he just looked at me. My first thought was, "Wow, that's four things." I thought to myself, "Lord please don't give me four things, just give me one, because I'm not able!"

Well, I soon had my share of more issues which made me take more notes, reflect on what wasn't working and how to fix it. I always came back to the people. I blamed my team for some of the shortcomings I found, but blame is not the answer. I didn't have a relationship with each of the team members. I thought I knew them because of their work habits and whatever personal information they shared with me.

Amazingly, when I took time to get to know them and they told me who they are outside of work, I saw them differently. Our dialogue improved, our relationships improved, they told me things that I didn't know, and some things about me that I didn't agree with, but at least now they were comfortable enough to share this.

They weren't wrong because that's how they perceived me. We went on to have great back-to-back-to-back months with the same resources and the same timelines. It wasn't just that I got to know them. I looked at the things that I needed to do to support them. I identified what I call *The Epaulettes of Leadership*.

Humble

Humility is not gratitude. The latter is case specific while the former is a way to live. How difficult is it to have humility? Is it something we try to obtain or thing we try to shun?

Your feelings can't feed your belly – eat your feelings, swallow your pride and get to work. Honest and true – it's that important!

Being humble should make you feel good, however, if you said, "I did a good thing today!" That's your ego, and it's not really humility. Being humble is putting others before you, and then they're better off. On your team, you're putting your teams' accomplishments before your own.

Don't get caught up in the trappings of your position. Do think back to your first day you got promoted, think about the interview, the night before the interview, and remember when you first discovered when you learned the position was available. What did you feel like?

There are too many what if scenarios to ignore. Things could have been different for you. I know it's sometimes hard to remember where we came from. I'm not referring to our hometown. Humility can help us keep ego at bay. Now, think about the people you are responsible for – they have families. If you lead with purpose they will follow with purpose. What you teach your people at work they can teach to their families.

Not in My House

I've worked with residents of homeless shelters. So many of them humble themselves based on where they reside. I caution them that home is not where you keep your stuff. This is where you're domiciled.

Your home is where you spend most of your time, and that is in your mind.

Since this is where we truly live, we should be carful as to how we furnish our homes. We can't bring in old, outdated, antiquated modes of thinking. If we often think about conditions that can't change, that's broken furniture we can't use.

We should be careful as to whom we let into our homes. Some people stop by to visit, but stay a long time. If they're not a part of our household, they shouldn't live in our home. Clutter in our homes can be cleaned out, but we'll have to decide what we need to part with.

When we humble ourselves it's not to crush our ego, we curb it. We ensure that we don't exalt ourselves over others. Unfortunately, some of us are hoarders of bad memories.

It's your home take it back.

Gentle Reminder: The best way to be humble is to be grateful.

Teachable

New supervisors should be coached first, and then mentored specifically for leadership. Start training by asking how they feel about their new position, responsibilities and their team. This is important, as they will need time to share concerns and maybe even fears. Listen, people need to share what they're feeling – you need to know how they feel!

Get this, you're coaching their feelings and mentoring their thoughts.

Whatever they ask you is a segue to: How do you feel about that? If you asked them, "How do you feel about your promotion?" They could reply that they're department is understaffed.

Here, you'll acknowledge that they shared that, but politely insist that they tell you how they feel about this. This is critical because the words they choose can help you to develop a narrative to address this.

You may not be able to easily onboard more staff. Now, if they say they feel nervous that they will not make a goal due to this reason, you want to find out what the new supervisor typically does when they feel this way. The coach mindset says, "When we have feelings that can't produce positive results, we have to decide if we want to serve or sever them."

This planted seed would not be soon forgotten.

- Tell them their feelings matter.
- Let them know the logistics behind hiring.
- Ask them what they would want in a team member.
- Let them know that you are coaching them and that you will mentor them after that.
- Explain that you expect them to do the same for their team.
- Tell them that you will provide them with training on how to interview.
- Ask them if they ever faced a similar situation where there was lack of resources and prevailed.
- Do they have a contingency plan to offset the shortcoming until staffing is at the allotted levels?

But as a coach for this person, you can tell them that the company is aware of this, and this supervisor was hired to help remedy the situation. Of course, you'll want to circle back to them to see how they are doing after your talk.

Coaching a new leader will directly address the self/ego proposition. You must do this in order to help them avoid leading people to their ego which is a temptation they will face. They may want to show drastic improvements in order to prove that they are better than their predecessor. They may want to make a name for themselves at the expense of their team.

Mentoring a new leader will help them to develop their vision which directly supports their supervisor's vision.

You don't want to leave them to begin their work, and then try to make time to train them. This training must be prepared. It's important for a higher-ranking leader to do this. Least the new supervisor yield back to their predecessor for leadership training.

Don't get me wrong, it's fine to do this for the technical aspects of the work, but leadership training should come from the top, not the past. You don't want this new leader to adopt any failed dynamic or partial thinking. The closer the training is to the top of the organization the better. If you have one trainer that is tasked with training all new leaders this is most desirable.

Remember: you're coaching, and then mentoring, but ultimately leading them to a sustainable vision within the *Continuity of Leadership* that they were commissioned to lead others to.

Teach them about the *Epaulettes*. Give them the definition and give them practical and relatable examples. Ask them about current or past situations that you both can review with an overlay of the *Epaulette's*.

How you go about scheduling and administering this is a logistical concern, but this should not take place in front of the staff. I also don't think a day a quarter will help. If you know the effective date of the new leader, schedule them and the trainer to be together in advance of the start date.

Teaching is like leading in that you may have a preferred methodology to engage people, but due to the different ways that people receive, absorb, and retain information and instruction, you will have to adapt to them. If his is true for you in the role of teacher, this would also be true of the person who is teaching, you.

Teaching is hard. I taught jobseekers and I found that the method that worked best wasn't so much teaching as it was selling. The principles of job readiness training are the same. The delivery method is what makes the course work stand out.

In fact, in my classes I had job seekers that attended job readiness trainings prior to mine. Yet, most people hadn't retained information from those classes. I was determined to do something different and make an impact. I decided to treat the class like they were my new team. I set the tone for them, as you should.

I couldn't let them do this for us because we would end up with as many tones as there were people present. Remember landlines? If you pressed one key you heard a distinct tone, but if you pressed more than one key at the same time, you would hear a combination of tones that didn't sound right.

I set the tone. Now, I must set the expectations for us with as much input from them as I can allow. Some would probably start the class with a thirty second pitch or resume, but not me.

I taught *Emotional Intelligence*, as this is critical for relationship success.

As a facilitator for job readiness workshops, I saw teaching as selling. I knew that anyone could come in and teach the course. You can find YouTube videos on the subject, what made me different was that I understand that job readiness/work readiness is best consumed via a sales delivery after exposing the emotion of your job seekers.

People who are unemployed, under employed, and have a history of poverty, experience their situation through their feelings. Every day I heard the issues that they had.

The job seekers would quickly tell me about how badly the system is run . I went right in there and told them how much experience I have. I quickly realized that this alone didn't garner the attention that I was looking for. I needed to get them to be receptive to my message.

It was only when I offered that my mom was once homeless. It was only for a short time, but I needed to let them know that I could identify with them. You can't teach people that are closed off to you. I found that in order to get them into receiving mode and to remember my message I had to appeal to their emotions.

I often tell people that you sell to emotions and rationalize the sale with their intellect. Our feelings tend to follow our thinking. We think bad, we feel bad. I understood that my position in their lives wasn't just to get them ready for a job – it was to prepare them for the things they wanted and loved out of life. It was to resolve the fear that they had about their situation and the future.

In these trainings it's often the customer we ask, "Where do you see yourself in five years from now?" It makes sense, as this is a popular employer question. But I found it more useful to ask, "Where do you see yourself five months from now and five days from now?" I had to lead them to a better place in their lives. Yes, this would require me to teach them.

Here's an exercise you can try. See if you can implement all seven *Epaulettes* into supervision sessions with your staff. If you can demonstrate how you used the *Epaulettes* for them, you can encourage them to do the same with those the lead.

Teaching will afford you the opportunity to use the methodologies as leading. You're coaching, mentoring, and selling. Coaching under the *Teaching Epaulette* means you will work to find out how the person learns and to work with that approach. While mentoring will test their knowledge and resolve. For teaching, you must sell first.

Explain the importance and relatability of the lesson. You're teaching the person how to teach.

What's the cost of bad morale?

Bad to the Bone

We can learn from things that go wrong, but we shouldn't let bad situations and experiences teach us. I mean we shouldn't come out of a bad experience and say, "I'll never trust again!"

What we can do is look at why the situation went bad – look at what was done or what wasn't done. What led up to that point?

I think rejecting the next opportunity will cost us a chance to implement a better plan. I marvel at people who don't take the opportunity to learn, because I don't understand why they do this. I've had staff that should have known how to punch-in and approve their timesheets, but they would forget every pay period. If you're a supervisor and must send out reminders to your staff to approve their timesheets you know what I mean. If you're that staff member, seriously?

We know it's not that the staff doesn't care – they want to get paid. I guarantee that if you have this problem, your staff will entertain similar problems, if you entertain it all then you're the host/hostess of that problem. They get to eat, leave their plate at the table, leave their chair out, and leave you to clean up. Still, some supervisors are okay with this. This may not be the biggest issue you have, but correcting it will help you to eliminate or mitigate similar shortcomings.

I tried to do things to help them remember, but this is not about memory or tricks used to remember, it's about learning how and why it's important to make correction.

Use themes to train your staff. They can play a major role in the culture of your organization. I like *Motivated Monday's*. This is where I made it a point to greet individuals in their workspace, talk to them, ask about their weekend, and share a motivational quote.

You know, if you don't set the tone for the team, especially on a Monday, you leave the team open to develop their tone. It's not that you can't trust the team, but you can't take the chance. I tried snack breaks with healthy snacks. That never went over well. Bless their hearts – my teams loved popcorn, chips, and sweets. So, I did that, and while we ate, I engaged them with work related questions. Sometimes I used the five-minute snack break to find out if everyone remembered an important date.

I think it's important to add extras to the relationship we have with our team. Imagine if it were a personal relationship and all you did was ask your significant other if they took care of something. People want to feel special. They don't want to be taken for granted. I even had some of my team dress with a theme-color for special occasions. Not everyone liked the color choice, and some complained that it was corny, but it got them all talking about the same thing.

You see, what you create for your team is uniquely yours and theirs. What you create for work is for the company. Well, that's how they see it. The day of the event you could see how powerful we were in sheer number due to the unspoken unity of the appearance of our outfits. Navy seal Admiral, William H. McRaven, shared that something as simple as making up your bed daily can change your life.

Well, if it's good enough for a SEAL, it's good enough for me.

Square Root of the Problem

Poor team morale is often derived from poor leadership, that is the person or persons that are appointed to leadership positions, but are not operating in leadership. Both poor morale and poor leadership can function independently of each other. If you have no knowledge of a matter, how can you base plans on it? I don't say this is the end all of leadership books, it's just one of many, but to continue to lead others without studying leadership and relationships will cripple your organization from the top.

Compassionate

Emotional Intelligence gives us a space to respond before we react and shrink the space of time to circle back and reverse ourselves if we are in error. This can save us a lot of heartache. Get a situation wrong, fail to understand why, and as a result let too much time pass, then you make way for a devalued relationship. You know, as an American, you get to enjoy the fruits of democracy, like saying, "I disagree with my leaders!" But with that comes a freedom to ferment the fruit, to get drunk on the freedom, to bottle it, and to label it.

There are a lot of workers who seemingly want to be at odds with their leaders. Therefore, I believe everyone should be taught leadership, as this will give us all a greater appreciation for those appointed over us.

Emotional Intelligence, or EI, is:

- **The study our emotions**
- **How to manage our emotions**
- **How others feel**
- **How to empathize with others**
- **And how to avoid conflict**

Showing compassion for others especially those you lead is essential for their well being, your vision, and just GP. But there is something weird about people who are hard and difficult. We don't immediately leave them. It's like we stick around to complain.

Have you ever seen what you would call a bad example of leadership? Some people will complain and others will explain it away. We shared a lot about what leadership is and how to apply it, but the leader is also an example to others.

We have to learn from our mistakes too. We need an incredible capacity to identify our own shortcomings by evaluating our performance. Sometimes we may have to bring these situations to a mentor (someone impartial that had a similar experience) to help us.

We don't know what we don't know and operating in ignorance is not a good excuse if we want to be the best leader for our people.

It's human to make mistakes, it's human to feel, and it is human feel angry. Now, if I feel angry and I think angry thoughts, this can translate into angry actions – this is human. Now, if I feel angry and I think positive thoughts, I'm a professional because I can still do the job.

Don't get me wrong, many people can have angry thoughts and still do their job, but the process of talking yourself through the difficulty is growth.

Example: the customer said something to make me angry – what can I do to deescalate the situation? How can I leave this situation without losing this customer? To give in to our feelings here would deny us growth into the next position.

As long as we are the employee, we are in the position to lead the situation. We can't mentor an upset customer because they're talking with their feelings, and so we must coach them. In the end, the example we set may satisfy the mentor part of this equation. It's not necessary to directly mentor every person we coach.

In the situation I just shared there wouldn't be enough time to directly do both, but we'll just have to be satisfied with the fact that we grew, and the customer saw an example of self-control and compassion.

I'll stay with the last example but go a little deeper. Not everyone will have received this type of training. If the person in this case, a customer, is quick to get upset, it could be that they are having a bad day, or they usually keep their feelings on the surface or just beneath it – that's a thick skin. Effective coaching cleans your skin, while effective mentoring will thicken your skin.

Compassion calls for a thick skin. Sure, we can be compassionate for someone that is terminally ill, but can we be as compassionate for someone that's willfully ill? The customer may not be right, but we still must lead the situation right.

To be clear, we will lead the situation by leading the person via that same person's feelings. Therefore, it's important to know how they feel about a given situation. People want you to fight for them and if need be, suffer with them too.

Do this: Put a name and a face to the work you do. Take time to talk to the people you lead. Get to know them, as many as you can, with meaningful conversation. This is better than just putting a valuation on your work. Valuation keeps you chasing after metrics at the expense of the people you lead to make your numbers work.

The meaning of the word compassion is to suffer with. It's a powerful word.

What's your relationship to X or Y?

Let's look at a relationship between the two letters X and Y. Algebra tells us that X and Y are in a linear relationship, because they're on the same line. Let's also use this rule for a certain couple. Now, X and Y will represent each of the partners. We have a nice example, but their values are unknown, and they can change. I know, equal is the most desirable equation because it's simple.

Let's say this couple has a falling out which changes their values. We have an equation, a problem, but they're still in the relationship because they're still on the same line. In order to make the equation true, they need to return to the original values in order to reach a solution. The conclusion to the matter must come from their ability to change for the solution because math doesn't lie.

I was one of those people that complained about always apologizing or opening discussions with my significant other after a falling out. Well, this just might be, but we should understand that we may have to lead that part of the relationship. Get over it. Don't expect co-leadership in the most difficult parts of your personal relationships. It is work for you, but your significant other ceded responsibility to this part of the relationship. You should find out why, but until you get the answer lead the shortcoming.

Gentle Reminder: Make it easy for people to work with you and they will want to work for you.

Communicators

> *It's not what you say – it's how you say it.*

Let's add: it's also when you say it.

One day my son asked me why I didn't marry his mother. I couldn't tell him my truth (his mother has her truth), because that's his mommy. It wasn't that she is a bad person, we just couldn't meet on common ground enough, or stay there long if we could find it. Well, he asked me this question while we were crossing the street one day. I told him, "We're crossing the street, and you can't ask me something like that right now!" He was like, "Oh, sorry!" Once we did cross the street, I offered him ice cream and he forgot about his question. I would say he is not mature enough to understand, but some people might say that I'm not mature enough to explain this to him. Finding the right words is not always easy.

The best communicators are the ones that tap into what we feel and make us think.

Politicians are great at doing this. They scare you into thinking you can lose something, and they paint a picture of what life will be like without it. They'll even give you a brief bio on some random person that contacted them personally and asked the candidate for help.

But not all great communicators are created equal. Some are great orators and other are great writers. Steve Maraboli is said to be the most quoted man alive. You don't get the distinction of that title without touching the feelings and minds of others. The best questions are the ones that people themselves would like to ask. If you ask these questions, it's like standing proxy for them and they want to know if you have the answer. People like Bishop T.D. Jakes comes to mind. Preachers by virtue of their work can speak to all parts of us.

Communication is about relationships, or perceived relationships, with others. Additionally, we want to lead people with communication. First, we start with the people. What is the purpose of the communication? What will this take? This is important because if where you intend to take them is far from where they currently are, you'd have to put in a lot more work.

List their takeaways – for you these are your talking points. An easy way to prepare this and easy for the audience is to make a relatable story out of the narrative. This is how you setup the connection to their feelings.

Okay, that works for presentations, but what about your everyday communications? How do you communicate directives and disseminate information? It's so interesting to me how quickly people can forget or misunderstand. I've learned to be extremely granular when providing information.

When sending emails, I use the same format. I start with a short paragraph to open, place the deadline by itself, followed by bulleted points.

The coaching plan should consist of:

- Where the person is supposed to be
- Where they are
- Suggestions for improvement
- Or congratulations for a job well done
- Where they land on the metrics for their position
- Can also include, but not be limited to, some professional development items
- Redirecting of unproductive energy
- And coaching of their emotions

Up to this point you covered the work part of the worker. Now, you can allow a space of time for the er part.

Also – encourage them to share any personal interests or pursuits they're working on. You'd be surprised at how talented your people are.

You can be a great communicator, but maybe your audience is not that great at receiving information. Communications with direct reports would benefit from coaching on your part. During some of your team meetings, coach them on *Active Listening*. There are plenty of amusing exercises on the internet. I like using customer examples that are long. This way I can see who is following, who is struggling, and how they respond to that example. The answer is usually simple and can be easily overlooked. People have surprising powers of recollection for details when the matter is of importance to them.

Whose House is This?

Let's look at another **example**: outside is work, but in the same town. If I'm a husband and my wife will only see me for my responsibilities and does not address the man that I am, I'm in trouble. As there is no effort to get to know me, the only relationship to be had is with my responsibilities.

Luther Vandross said, "A house is not a home." I would add, "and a home is not a relationship!"

Since I'm on the topic of relationships and homes, I'll borrow a home remodeling term to explain this next point. I call it *Open Concept Relationships*. Open concept is the removal of walls and barriers that define distinctly and succinctly different parts of a home. Why can't we apply this same methodology to relationships?

This works best when both parties actively look to remove barriers early in the relationship. Failure to jointly remove barriers or an uncooperative partner could likely lead to a breakup. That's fine because this is better than living in a home with more walls that livable space.

Question: if you can't take the walls down and you're not happy, why stay? What happens in these situations is the parties end up living in their respective quarters, activities, their minds, and their finances, until they become roommates in the home of their relationship. They need space to grow. As I said in *Leadership Epaulette*: Humble, home is where your mind is. In the example I just shared, there is a maturity that is needed because the walls of the relationship are an extension of the walls in their minds.

Maturity is growth!

Grow for It

> *You will have disastrous results if you grow the work before growing the worker.*

They will resent you for it. By coaching their emotions, presenting opportunities for short informal professional development, and let them share what's on their mind, you can truly grow them. It's only after this is imitated with a measure of success that you should add more work.

The examples above nicely match this example. I'm sure you would purchase clothing for your child that is a size larger, so they can grow into them, right? Likewise, prepare your people for growth before you demand or require it from them. While you're at it, ensure that you have grown in a complementary way as well to lead and support them.

Gentle Reminder: People give you the perspective of leadership and you give them the perspective of vision.

Back to the Beginning

It seems the serpent had more dialogue (communication) with Eve than Adam did. At the very least, what the serpent told Eve was actionable. There is no record of Adam telling her something and her doing it. When she was tempted, she references God, which is good, but never her husband. I find that interesting. We learned the serpent cross-coached her to commit an act that was counter to her orders and be default the *Continuity of Leadership Chain*. I'm sure Adam had more to say to Eve, but he may not have coached her.

You see, your team will be bombarded by coaches with agendas. As a leader, you must create and maintain a program of coaching with communication at its core. Adam may have thought that because they were in a relationship, things were okay. But relationships are work, and if you are in a relationship you become a work(er). This is another reason why the leader should spend most of his or her time coaching.

Now, I want to make a case for effective communicating. Eve told the serpent that if she ate of the tree of Good and Evil she would surely die. That's not the command that God gave them. Okay, people get things mixed up, but Adam could have coached her by asking, "How do you feel about the tree of the knowledge of good and evil?" Whatever her response, he had to coach for that.

If you lead people, you know this all too well – you will remind, reinforce, recondition, and reposition them.

Feedback is a Tool – Not a Weapon

Offering feedback is a good thing but this can go badly if it is delivered incorrectly.

Feedback is the last stage in the life cycle of any project or task, and it should be the beginning of the next project or task. When delivered correctly, it should inspire to improve something and/or avoid something.

I want to make the problem the problem, and not the person the problem. If I said, "You did this wrong," the message can be perceived as personal attack. First, I want to make mention of the person's effort, point out the shortcoming, and then ask how we can do this differently next time. I isolate the shortcoming and compare it to the desired outcome.

Now, I can't attack the outcome because the person it belongs to could be proud of the effort they put into it. I must employ *Allied Leadership* by coaching and mentoring this person. I will start with, "How do you explain where we are today in relation to where we should be?" And then, I want to ask about setup, preparation, expectations, resources, timing, and planning.

If I made an outline of these areas prior to assigning the project or task, then we can trace back to the source together. This is important, as I don't want the person to perceive me as Superior Shawn, always finding fault. I want a substantive analysis of the situation that we both can look at and agree upon. This is not a case where I listen to my gut. The proof is in the pudding! This means we'll have to eat the pudding to get the proof. And so, the pudding feedback should be palatable.

Feedback in personal relationships is important for individual growth as well as the growth of the union.

However, I don't think the feedback we have for them should be reserved for when they give us feedback – that's a fight! But why do we hold onto feedback we should share in the first place? It's usually because we think our feedback may create a fight. Okay, but why give feedback after we receive feedback? Wouldn't this still cause a fight?

Well, it's because now we believe we're in a fight, and so there is no reason to save it. The hope is that the relationship had grown to the point where it can shoulder feedback. Now, if you thought withholding feedback is the way to go, you would be wrong because this also means that you're not willing to grow the relationship or yourself.

Coaching and Mentoring Work Relationships

When providing feedback from the coaching mindset, we're concerned with how the person is feeling because we may have to address some shortcoming, and we want them to have the courage and hope to try again. We're not trying to be the subject matter expert – we are trying to be their advocate.

Buy the Rumor – Sell the News

How does your team perceive you – would they call you a complainer or a campaigner?

All strategy involves the movement of people in response to defend, attack, supply, think, purchase, vote, strike, play, help, sell, give, etc. Sometimes we're directed to, or direct others, to take the actions above and are conditionally bound to them, if directed to do so. But what about those of us that are not?

I rarely write about politics, but I feel that I must make this comparison in a *Seven Epaulettes* way. The American political system is dominated by two political parties. They are the Republicans and the Democrats. The Republicans are the party of current president Donald Trump. Democrats may define President Trump as someone with a devil-may-care attitude as he doesn't seem to be concerned with the consequences of his actions.

They'll call him out on this, but this doesn't seem to work for the public. It's like riding in a car with a driver that got cut off and for fifteen minutes, they complain about the bad driver. They say things like, "Can you believe what that driver just did?" "Where are the police, why don't they have cameras here?" Initially, you, the passenger, would agree with the driver. Well, for the first four seconds, but then you have moved on and the driver is still committed to the long-over situation.

Now, the passenger will begin to ignore the driver and subsequent trips will become arduous. Remember, the bad driver is now gone. And so, I submit to you, that there is a fine line between complaining and campaigning. Well, for most people anyway.

> *Campaigning is talking about what others want and complaining is talking about what we want.*

If you're the driver, you have the means to steer as many people as can fit in your vehicle. Spend too much time concerned with people outside of your vehicle and you may find yourself driving alone. Take solace in the fact that your former passengers wouldn't join the bad driver – no, they don't do that.

Republicans are still conservative, but Democrats are still traditional. Their narrative is predictable, and it serves the party, but not so much the people. And I say this with respect to both parties. For Democrats to get their passengers back, they would have to realize that you cannot check a pulse with the back of your finger. The same is true for you and your organization.

Complaining to people about things you have the power to change will turn them off. How can you lead people, and then tell them it's up to them? I know, we're talking about voters! They must vote to make change, but they voted you into office and gave you the power to do what they collectively couldn't manage.

The short of it is this: Managers complain and leaders campaign.

I especially like the theme of campaigning. It's a specific form of sustained coaching for a group of people making or maintaining change. This will be different from cross coaching, as this method will benefit a group over and above that of the leader.

The more we study people the more forgiving we will be. People will let us down – it's inevitable, they're human. People don't generally want to fail. Success is synonymous with survival. The threat of failure makes people believe survival is elsewhere. It never is because they're trying to physically retreat to their ego. If we say failure or defeat is physical and inevitable, they'll curl up into the fetal position.

We may be equipped to manage or lead success, but can we manage failure? What's your knee jerk reaction to the prospect of failure? Do you look to find the issue, find fault, double up your efforts, or cut your losses and move on?

It's case specific but what you initially do is what will lead you. Before you react wait, the wrong move could make things worse. Why do you want to take a particular action? Is your action ego-driven? It would be better to respond. You led your team up to this point – don't abandon them now.

Punishment in failure isn't good either. You'll have to take stock of what was lost and what is left. Coach your team through this difficult time. Find out what worked no matter how insignificant and eliminate what didn't work. Don't point fingers or allow your team to point fingers, this will divide them. It may not play out publicly but believe me they will have an opinion and discuss it amongst themselves.

Gentle Reminder: Don't look for opportunities – find them!

What happens when only some of your team is performing to standard? For all intents and purposes, you have two teams. You can spend more time coaching the lower performers and more time mentoring the high performers. And, you still need to make time to bring all of them together.

I split my team into teams often, and then appointed team leads. This took some pressure off me to be everywhere. Rather than do a lot of general leadership type functions. I spent time working closely with them one-on-one when I could. I didn't like setting up everyone with assignments and walking away knowing some other them were still struggling. It worked out fine because I put my leadership into the relationships I had with each of them.

Don't lower your eyes at your opponents. Instead, lower your head, or they will humble you. Being big and powerful will establish you by the rules of the game, but your opponents who would take your eyes as disrespect, will soon forget their source of contention with you, which could have been ideology, preferences, etc. Now, they will make this personal and try to destroy you.

Gentle Reminder: Anything that doesn't profit you will cost you.

Visionary

The work is not in the vision – it's in your relationship to your vision.

There are two types of vision.

Tepid vision is like rubbernecking a car accident. You have a picture of what's going on, you have an interest to know more, but you're not doing anything to affect the situation. This is also called a dream because you can't interact with it.

Sighted vision is a picture that you create. It's the big picture with action taken to materialize it, which is vision.

Your vision is more than a picture. A picture is a snapshot of what the future can look like. Well, what do we do with a picture that we like? We frame it! If this is mistaken for the vision, the work would stop.

Imagine a shop where the leader has no vision and as a result, he or she cannot help their team to develop their respective visions of what they need to do. Now, they have a shop full of people with no vision. Early in our reading we learned that without vision, leaders lead people to their egos. Well, the same is true of the leaders direct reports. They will lead their work and responsibilities to their egos without leadership. Therefore, we need to teach them leadership as well.

Good relationships produce good work and good work produces good outcomes – this is a perpetuating cycle. This is behind the love-work, work-love logo on the cover of this book.

An unobstructed view of your vision is critical for you to stay ahead of the curve. It's frustrating for workers to get hit with, "You have to double your output right away, or we'll no longer have access to a particular support." And not understand why, or believe that, you should have foreseen this before it snuck up on them. There is no such thing as *Per Diem Leadership*, but we can define the effects of such a phenomenon just as scientists can define a black hole without having seen one. This is a manager that leads on demand. Not particularly concerned with anything or anyone beyond today's goal.

So far, I referred to vision as a positive thing to have. It would not be uncommon for someone to have a vision that is not of a positive nature. What they see and determine to materialize could have success, but could also create havoc for others.

Every great innovation, breakthrough, and accomplishment was first seen by a leader and their relationship to their vision. Ford had the idea of an affordable car for the masses – this was a good thing.

Franz Reichelt, a French tailor, had a fatal relationship to his vision. His claim to fame was his jump, by parachute, from the Eiffel Tower. Get this, he jumped in a parachute that he created himself. Okay, he was a tailor and he had tinkered with various models. As a former paratrooper, I appreciate this man's effort, but it should not have cost him his life. He had a vision of a device that could save lives – how noble! He jumped into a relationship with a great vision that, for him, was flawed.

There's a scene in *Forrest Gump* where Forrest is running on a road. He shares that he's been running for over three years, and just like that he decides to stop running, even with a clear road ahead of him and dozens of people following. He declares, "I'm tired, I want to go home." One of those runners asks, "What are we going to do now?"

Just like that people can run right out of their vision. In this case, the vision had a purpose, but it wasn't defined, and so Forrest just kept running. While this was work and things were happening, people were joining it. In this case he wasn't leading them. He was more influencing them. Recall how he didn't coach or mentor anyone.

This happens outside of the movies too. Some people want to be a part of a movement. Be careful leaders – justify your vision with purpose. And because this is my book, I think more leadership is needed for the purposes of helping others. People who lack the means to achieve and maintain a quality of life that will sustain themselves and their immediate households need more leadership. No, not socialism. I do think that those who risk more and sacrifice more should have more, but they should also give more.

I believe this is societal leadership. It is kinetic in nature because its force creates opportunity and motivates their peers and near peers to emulate them. I don't knock captains of industry who amassed great wealth first and then used it to help others. I'm okay with this as the distribution of their wealth has and will continue to benefit millions of people.

Leader Application – I must firstly vet my vision.

- Does my vision line up with the vision of the person I report to, or is it contrary?
- If my vision is not lining up, I need to speak with my boss.
- If I'm not sure, I should talk to my boss.
- If I'm sure my vision lines up with my boss I should still inquire.
- How well do I know my team?
- How well do I know what they are facing now?
- And what will they face as we proceed?

Share the vision with those you lead, but put that vision inside of a culture. To those that follow, this will become a way of life, something to buy into, and more importantly, something to support. Failure to do this makes your vision a chore and a bore.

Make the vision more than a goal. Make it an exciting way to live. I can incorporate things that we can do right now that aren't necessarily work, but I can tie them into the vision. I don't think it would be wise to say, "This is my vision, and because I am your manager/supervisor you have to do this!" Well, that's what some leaders sound like. How can fulfilling your vision change their lives? Not just in the future when it materializes, but right now.

When I recorded my first YouTube video, I was nervous. I knew the endeavor would bring success.

I was so nervous I couldn't remember the lines I wrote. It took me dozens of take and retakes to do ten minutes.

Gentle Reminder: The future was bought today and everyday pays for the future.

This is interesting in that you see your vision firmly planted in the future and yet every day you must move towards it. Add to that the people that are involved with your vision, you must move them forward too. In other words, your commitment to what you see, which hasn't happened yet, is how you bought it.

Example: you decide to get married. You tell people, you save money, you spend money on wedding items, you plan for a wedding, and you tell people about your plans. Finally, you invite some of those people to join you in the wedding and the planning for the wedding. You will naturally give all involved updates and information, but you know that in order to maintain and realize the vision you have for the wedding, you will continuously sell it to them. You describe details from your mind's eye. And some of those people will say, "Yes, I see it too!"

Now, these are your people that you know. What about the people you work with? You don't know them as well, and maybe you wouldn't have picked this iteration of the team. How do you get people to see your vision? Make it a wedding. They should know you or at least feel like they know you. Make the endeavor exciting and give them a special place at the wedding - you're coaching them.

Can a stranger walk up to you and invite you to their wedding? No, there's no commitment to you. I once used an example of no relationship – no commitment with a cashier. You order food from a quick service restaurant and the cashier can be nice to you, but they're not committed to you because they don't know you.

Now, after visiting the same establishment daily you develop a rapport. The cashier now feels committed to you and will act on this with small gestures like circling back to a previous discussion with you. This shows they paid attention.

If you are getting married to someone, I'm sure you both have this image (vision) of what marriage will look like for you. Now, if you could take your vision of marriage and their vision of marriage and put them side-by-side, would the pictures match, would they complement each other? Or, would they badly contrast?

Vision is what you develop by virtue of your purpose.

It should not be mistaken with a dream which originates from you. I said a lot right there. People dream about a happy ending in a big house with the perfect mate. They dream about owning multiple homes and having wealth. Your dream is derived from your ego. Leaders shouldn't waste time dreaming, as it may be hard for some to distinguish a dream from a vision. Sure, you could say that your dream to attain wealth will put you in a great position to help others. So, while your purpose is yours, it's given to you, and you get to create the vision for that purpose.

Example: the purpose of a door is not to be a door. It's a barrier, used to allow or deny access to a space. If you think your purpose is about you, then you would have no more effect on your purpose than a door would on the space before and after it. That's like saying a fault in a lock that is difficult to open is itself a security feature.

A vision will not always come with a plan, and don't fool yourself into thinking that because you have the vision you will have the plan as well. There are people who work in operations that figure out how to make everything flow.

Resilient

In most cases, you can affect a situation, whereas a condition cannot be changed so easily.

A situation is something you can enter. You can walk into it. This may not have been voluntary, but you have some degree of control as it relates to exiting the situation. A condition is something that is difficult for you to change.

I had friend with a child that had a motor tick. The child would turn his head impulsively. At first the tick surfaced every ten minutes or so. The father, wanting to help his child, or so he thought, made a point of telling the child every time the tick was evident.

It turns out these kinds of ticks are hereditary. It was discovered that the child's mother had it and apparently it went away on its own. My friend did not live with his child and the child's mother. More than a week passed before he could see a neurologist. The mother never mentioned during this time that she once had it. This information only came out when the neurologist shared that the tick is hereditary and had to have come from one of the parent's lines.

The child's mother believed people have ticks and it's not a big deal. To my friend, who had no experience with it, became obsessed with it. He prayed for change often and seemed depressed about it. This was all before the neurologist visit.

Now, after it was determined that no treatment was needed and the child would grow out of it on his own, my friend relaxed. What was interesting was the neurologist shared that anxiety and stress can bring on the ticks. It was then that my friend realized that he was causing the tick to appear more frequently by bringing it to his child's attention. His son would look at his father after the tick appeared, fearing the father would comment.

The tick is an example of a condition that we cannot change. The tick was inside the child. Watch this, my friend would point out every instance where the tick presented itself to his son. My friend was reacting instead of responding. And, in that case, without knowing it, he exasperated the situation. What's also important to note is his son's mother treated the condition as if it were a situation. The good news is tick went away for a whole week before it appeared again a few times.

Well, if it's possible to perceive or treat a condition like a situation, then it's possible to perceive a situation as a condition. In the instance, we're making more out of the situation. In my friend's case, he projected his fears, insecurities, and frustration onto his son. When we make a situation a condition, we project all that is negative onto ourselves. Don't let your insecurities get in the way of the work you have to do.

Example: if my team was fully staffed and underperforming, I have a situation here. But if my team is underperforming because we're understaffed, I have a condition. I don't know when I'll find that right fit someone. And, there's no guarantee that this person will make an impact right away.

Example: if someone had a bad marriage, that would have a situation as I they could divorce. But someone could argue that this is a condition as it would take some time to get out of the marriage and the effects of divorce may last longer than the marriage itself. I would give such an example a new designation. I would call it a Conditional Situation. In this case, the situation carries the condition. A clean, amicable, even-split, or windfall for one side would sever the situation, but the break would come with conditions, and this they will continue to live with. So you see, not every situation is one we can get out of.

How we deal with a situation can determine how we come out of a situation. We can walk out of it, run out of it, fight out of it, fall out of it, fail out of it, etc. Going from situation to situation is not good. That is, the very same situation every time! This itself could be the result of a condition.

Think about it, you've been here before. If this were a test, you erased all the wrong answers and replaced them with the same wrong answers. Did you do this? And then, you turned in your test and waited for the results. If this is you, you're human. If you feel badly and have regrets this is a natural response to trauma – self-inflicted trauma.

Don't give yourself pow-pow. You deserve better, you're 100% worth what you want. Explore and understand why this is happening. The people you lead deserve better too. They need you to lead yourself first, and then lead them. So, because we're leaders doesn't mean we have it all together. I'm okay with a leader that makes a mistake and has the desire to fix it. Mistakes help us to be humble, addressing our mistakes helps us to coach others better, and fixing our mistakes should give us more compassion for others. Close the distance.

So, we possess the epaulettes, and this is evident in our work and disposition, great! Up until now, we haven't discussed how difficult it is to present them all the time. You may get a reprieve as the leaders you train up, step in to shepherd some of the responsibilities, but you signed up for this. More importantly, leaders were made for this.

What about rebounding? For something to rebound, it must have impacted something else. In the case of the *Visionary Epaulette*, we saw French tailor and inventor, Franz Reichelt, jump from the Eiffel Tower with a parachute of his own design. His impact on parachute development was lasting as he is remembered for his effort, although, the impact he and his chute made was too great for him to survive. It was also too great for his form to rebound back to the pre-jump height.

Some leaders believe they should conform to their staff, while others believe the opposite. They not only believe, but also expect their staff to conform to them. I was one of these leaders. My thinking was, "I went through a lot to get here – people just don't know the half of it! Now that I have this position and the authority to correct all the wrongdoing I've seen, I can lead my staff to extraordinary feats," – I was so naive.

It's weird, but people want their leaders to do those extraordinary feats that I mentioned, yet they still want to know that their leader is human. We like it when our leaders can step in and fix a problem, but we also want them to ask for our input. We want them to be fair to a fault and we also want them to give us favor. We don't want our leaders to know our personal business, but we want to find ourselves in their inner circle – we like being in their inner circle – it makes us feel important.

Rock Bottom

They say if you hit the bottom it's not so bad because you can't go any lower. Well, there is worse than rock bottom! Say someone else is at rock bottom with you and one day you see them ascending.

Okay, we covered the coach and the mentor, but there is another mindset to be aware of. It belongs to people I call *coachy*. They speak as if they are mentors, but remember, mentors are not with you, telling you what to do, instead they call you to where they are. Furthermore, a coach will encourage you and inspire you, right there where you are.

A coachy person will tell you what to do and they make you feel entitlement. They give you a deadpan look and say, "If I were you, I would do this or that," but that same advice hasn't seemed to work for them. A coach conditions you by getting you to work on the parts before the sum-total, and this is not easy. A coachy person will tell you they have the answer but without effort. It's like a life hack – just do this!

Coachy people are just highly opinionated, not highly qualified. Now, let's address the fact that they tell you what you should do as if they are mentoring you. Coachy people don't have a place to take you or send you because they're right there with you. They're in the same station in life. I thought it important to mention this, as it can be easy to follow a voice in your ear that sounds like it belongs to a person that knows what they're saying. And, these voices are even more appealing when we have a decision to make. I don't doubt that some of these people are sincere, but for me, if you didn't do it, you can't prove it.

Some people coach from their emotions. This okay if this is their style, but coaching comes from experience. You played the game, you studied the game, and you have a measure of success.

Oh, my Epaulettes!

Nice guys finish last. If you do things to make people think you are nice you will be sorry. Instead do what is right. Some may think you are nice, and others may not – live with it!

In sales closing is great, but adjusting to make the sale is even better because this brings consistency. The same is true for leadership. We must adjust to internal and external changes. What worked an hour ago may not work now.

Why don't we study people we have relationships with the same way? How long has someone known you and yet they can't connect with you in the simplest of ways?

Some are too afraid or ashamed to disclose to you that they cannot maintain their end of the relationship. That's so unfortunate because if it were a true relationship in the first place, they could have shared this.

It's better to devalue a relationship with the other party versus allowing the relationship to degrade on its own. If something is devalued, and by that I mean to relax expectations of all parties involved, you have the option to rebuild. This may not be an open door, but at least you have something to work with. By contrast, if a relationship is left to degrade you lose parts of it. We may prefer it this way because it's uncomfortable to talk about how we feel. People love getting the job but not the work involved. Maintaining the job is a relationship. You longed for it, you asked for it, and you got it. Now, prove it, every day.

Gentle Reminder: Successful leaders communicate emotion and they impart intellect to their teams.

We often get this backwards. We might tell our team the importance of meeting goal this quarter. This is a logical approach, but people respond best to emotion.

One day while reviewing what I thought was a winning, in-action plan, it occurred to me that I had put the proverbial cart before the horse when I shared the plan with the team, and then I circled back to them to see how they were doing. I thought I was a thoughtful leader.

But when I asked them how they felt about the plan to meet the goal that I developed, I learned that some struggled with the viability of it. Others complained about variables that were out of my control. And a few distracted me with what was distracting them. I went back to my office thinking, "This is one team that's in pieces. I'm not sure how I missed so much of what's going on around me." Some of my people had personal issues that required me to just listen to them.

Okay, what do we do here? Have a meeting to rally the team? Speak with individuals one-on-one? Let everyone know that my door is always open to them? Yes, all the above, but this won't prevent this from happening again. After all, stuff happens, but it is possible to fulfill your obligations and responsibilities despite this.

This new approach may not mend all my pieces together, but at least they would be close enough to move the work along.

I decided to change the way I present and represent work to my team. I will firstly address their emotional needs leading into tasks and goals.

After that, I present the tasks or goals as a question, not a problem. That was the key – even the narrative had to be question driven.

Lastly, I shred the plan. This seems counter-intuitive as reflex would prompt you to lead with, "Team we have a big problem here!" I used the horse and cart, but let me use this example.

I think what I had been saying is team, "We're this close to making goal. We just have to keep pressing. We've been here before and we've exceeded the goal before. We don't need to remember what it takes to make a hundred, we just need to remember what makes one. Just keep making one and I'll keep score for you, but make the one the best one you can!"

Sounds okay, but I've used that so many times. You can't find enough creative ways to say this same thing. After a while people become immune to the message. And soon after that, immune to the messenger. This is another reason to lead your plan by taking the current team's emotional state into account.

They may need motivation, a period of reflection, a break, etc. Ideally, I must stay in tune to what's going on with them. Before I tell my team, "We're still short twenty-five of the goal for this month," I need to know what's on their minds.

In this example, the emotional state of your team is like that of railroad tracks. They can go left, right, up and down. And yes, your train will do the same as it travels along with them. Trains get updated, they can be late, and even breakdown, but tracks are a constant. They maintain their integrity to the ground and the linked track to either side of them.

Your leadership must be viewed by your team in the same way. Your a constant in the office, and by default in thier lives.

Kinetic Leadership

Kinetic Leadership is motivational.

This is often applied on a larger scale by politicians. You lead people to act based on some perceived or implied advantage, compensation, or entitlement. You're trying to make stark comparisons between your peers or near peers.

This is easier because you operate on a macro scale where it's difficult to produce tangible results. People most easily affected by this are those who may want to complain. Do you know that there are people who like complaining? If you ask them what they have done to change the situation that they dislike, they couldn't share anything with you.

They want to see that someone powerful identifies with them. They want the person to publicly say what they want to say. They want to live vicariously through this person. Most people who respond to this identify with someone who presents as passionate, but I would call them emotional. Don't get me wrong, kinetic leadership is not evil. This is one of those areas that if left unchecked or devoid of direction could lead to widespread chaos.

Kinetic leadership was employed by the serpent to influence Eve and its effects are still being felt to this day. In fact, the Bible says he beguiled her. To beguile is to charm, and so this is the first instance where the charismatic form of leadership was used. In this context, his form of leadership was not in telling her what to do. It was in influencing her as to what she should do.

Remember, he wasn't a part of the *Continuity of Leadership Chain*. We should always be aware of these types of leaders as they can pick off members of our team.

Kinetic energy is force and you will use the force of emotions to emotionally force people into action.

People who operate with this kind of leadership can easily tap into the emotions of others.

This is the most important form of leadership as this kind of leadership will get people to act, and proximity is not a factor for people like static leadership. A great deal of charisma is need here.

People want the vision because you sold it to them, and they want you because you sold it to them. What does it take to get people to act? You must get them to feel something. The same is true of bringing change.

Initially, areas of concern may not always be identifiable, until you begin kinetic leadership. You're trying to get people to act, beyond what is obvious. It's getting them to take more than action, it's getting them to shepherd the responsibilities you entrusted them with.

This is often when friction-points surface. They consist of people who will not follow due to their dislike of the changes or not understanding them. Removal of the friction points is not removal of the person and it's coaching those feelings for them. If they have a problem, it's because they feel something. Policy, procedures, threats or treats won't change this for them.

Same Difference

Supervisors need an internal conflict training guideline to follow as one small situation can have big repercussions. Imagine if multiple supervisors address conflicts on their teams. None of these supervisors received formal leadership training, they mean well, and resolve their respective situations based on their critical thinking.

Do you think all will be resolved completed? Okay, this sounds like a loaded question, but how do you know? They could end up with as many results as there are situations. And, who's to say that they will repeat the same process that led them to the outcome.

Since we know there will be conflict at some point, we should equip our supervisors with an outline to contain, mitigate, and resolve conflicts.

Not only are the supervisor's critical thinking skills different, but so are their cultures, religious beliefs, discernment, tolerance, etc. Such a guideline would be in addition to the company handbook. It's called a leader's handbook.

Teachers are Worth Their Weight in Gold!

I've had leadership assignments where I led soldiers, and then soldiers and civilians, small teams in corporate, small teams in nonprofits, large teams, large teams across multiple locations, and, by far the most difficult group of people to lead were, job seekers in one classroom.

I have a unique way of connecting to people. No pretenses, no judgment, but I do cover nuances that are difficult to articulate and topics that carry stigmas. It's often what we are uncomfortable talking about is what we need to talk about. Even when I teach people I use direct and indirect methods, but both can't be denied by the student – I'll teach you to your face!

This simply means that you can't ignore it. I want to illicit emotions. Remember, I'm leading their emotions and managing their intellect. This work cannot be done without touching the emotions. People are usually busy thinking they're so smart. And, they want to you how real they are, and how important that is to them.

I get it, you have a measure of success, but for the next station in your life you need a coach and a mentor. These words can be a turn off, but who better to take you to the next level? Why would you want to take advice from your barber or hairstylist?

Line of sight managing is a tool managers use to get people to work. And, this method only works if the manager is right where all the worker can see him or her watching. This method will result in the team resenting you. In fact, as soon as you leave they will talk about you, mock you, and maybe even undo some of the work they did.

Gentle Reminder: Look like your future.

I had a job as a facilitator for a job readiness program. My students were well intentioned, but collectively they lacked discipline and focus. It didn't take much to get them distracted, which forced me to steer them back. I addressed this problem by telling them to think about the person they want to be in the future. This is the vision they have of themselves. Then I told them that they needed to look like that person, today. I told them to look like their future.

I think everyone understood me that day, but not everyone received the thought. I employed a new methodology to this situation. I call it *Kinetic Influence*. Kinetic, because this represents movement. And influence, because this is my goal. And so, if this approach worked, I would successfully influence them to not only hear and listen to me, but my influence would move them to act.

Professionals recognize the difference between what they feel and what they think. And they make appropriate decisions. Leaders not only do this, but they influence others to do the same. Both leaders and professionals will act in this way consistently.

We start out with a picture in our mind's eye of what we want. It's our vision. We know leaders must have a vision, but along the way to reaching that vision, life happens. Something goes wrong and now a piece of the vision breaks off. This by itself is not an issue, but in time more pieces will break away – it happens to all of us. We may not have taken notice of the first piece, but subsequent breaks that produce more pieces are too noticeable to miss.

Visionaries – this is more than just line-of-sight. This pierces through the fog of war. Visionaries look like their future! They see the big picture with detail, but they leave the details to be lived and worked out day-to-day. Perhaps Tesla's greatest experiment was his life. His was arguably the most brilliant genius of his time and yet he died a poor broken man.

Any team that is fully stocked, fully equipped, trained, motivated, disciplined, healthy, creative, mature, and emotionally well adjusted doesn't need a leader.

The point here is this: stop choosing because you inherited a team with shortcomings. Stop complaining about infighting, dysfunction, waste, lack of focus, and low morale. This is precisely why leaders were created.

When we're incapable of forging relationships with people it's easy to blame them. Set the expectation early in the relationship. Your ability to lead is what gravity is to closely orbit heavenly bodies. You can pull people in with your leadership and hold them in a priceless course, or your leadership can deflect them into deep space. Someone needs to pull the team together and then pull out.

This is another topic I covered previously, but it's one that's important enough to bring back. It's so important that I use it as my company motto:

Lead your purpose and manager your principles.

This narrative is directly related to work. I want you to lead what you are called or hired to do – this is our purpose. Principles are a train of thought we develop while we are engaged in our purpose.

Make it easy for other people to work with you.

Have you ever heard someone say, "I know a guy!"? This is generally a person that is agreeable, likeable, and ultimately productive.

This is not like being the nice guy. Nice guys do finish last because they want to be liked, often to their own detriment. You will be well liked if you let people take advantage of you and then refer their friends to take advantage of you as well. I prefer to be the right person versus the nice person.

On two occasions in my career I was to be trained or given information from a colleague. The information and trainings that I needed would be of vital importance to my success. On both occasions the colleagues assigned to me failed to provide me with what the supervisor had asked them to.

Of course, this was frustrating and neither fully offered the assistance. What I took from both those experiences was that I didn't need them after all. I was looking for something that someone didn't want to give me. How can I need something you won't give to me?

Instead of looking for what I needed in them, I found it elsewhere. I trained myself. This worked out better for me because I didn't know when to stop training myself. I trained myself well enough to become successful and in time I went on to train others. And, this is the conclusion of the matter.

Are your close associates talking to you about discounts on household items? Well, their aim is to maintain the nest that you created with them. I don't have a problem with this, but I want some talk and action of growing beyond the discount.

Parallel Planning

Gentle Reminder: Growth is a product of growth.

It never surprises how people are so consumed with growth at a company. In my line of work, I speak with job seekers daily and their number one question is about growth in a company. What makes matters worse is, I've had some colleagues that taught job seekers that this question is acceptable at interview.

How can you ask about growth when you didn't even get the job yet? That's like meeting someone for the first time today and asking them when you can go to their house. Well, the person would be alarmed because they don't know if they like you enough to see again.

It doesn't show initiative or motivation. You haven't proven yourself yet. Even if there was room for growth, there is no guarantee that you would be selected for a higher position.

You might disagree with me, but I have often facilitated job readiness trainings for job seekers that insisted in asking this question. Ironically, these same people would not challenge themselves to grow in the classroom. They would speak just fine about frivolous things not class related, but would shy away from public speaking. They would be last to participate, mock interviews and other opportunities to grow. How could they expect a company to invest in them beyond the initial position that they haven't secured, to address the matter of the next one?

Emotional Intelligence

I showed my class pictures of people with different facial expressions. They were able to identify the happy faces easily, but they were split when the faces where sad, confused, distrusting, etc.

Do this exercise with your team. A part of *Emotional Intelligence* is being able to understand someone else. If my class had such a hard time with facial expressions that weren't happy, it made me wonder how this would affect them at work. If they saw these facial expressions on the customers they were talking to, they may have missed opportunities to resolve issues, steer someone to buy, or know when it's time to fold em.

Now, this class was together for a period of weeks. They had the opportunity to be taught by me and we had done similar exercises. You would think that after being together they would have come to the same conclusions about the facial expressions more often. The fact that some got it right, some wrong, and others non-decided concerned me deeply.

Leading larger groups of people, or the same group of people with more responsibility, will call for more leadership skills. I think this is where many leaders go wrong. They instinctively look to become more technically proficient as they are elevated to positions of higher authority. And, every relationship must have someone to lead some aspect of it at some point – relationships without leadership are pointless.

When you get promoted, you are no longer the biggest part of your vision. Granted, you have successfully led yourself, now it's time to lead others. Your vision – what is before you, and your legacy – what is behind you, will depend on how well you not only lead others, but how you develop them as leaders.

Gentle Reminder: Career growth is supported by personal growth.

As you advance in the ranks and have more people under you, more of your focus is on the people. Quality of life, training, company culture, customer service, emotional intelligence, and operations are your focus. As you advance you also gain subordinate leaders who will manage more of the day-to-day team leading.

Your ability to occupy this part of the business will clear a path for the supervisor to lead the team through. Failure to do this will leave the team complaining. And once they feel their complaints are not being heard or heeded, their principles take hold.

Now, morale is affected, production is affected, execution of plan is sloppy. The lower performing percentile of your workforce will stay despite being unhappy, and the higher performing workers will see the writing on the wall and exit the company. It amazes me how some people will be bitterly upset with an employer, yet would not look for employment elsewhere.

Gentle Reminder: Change in the moment is for convenience. Change in the present is for the future.

Have you had this experience? You give someone constructive feedback and they say, "Yeah, I know, I'm working on changing that!" No, they weren't. They only said that to end the criticism.

So, they said that in the moment. Change in the present is doing something now, in advance of that shortcoming to mitigate it. The next time someone tells you they're working on it, ask them what does that look like and how is that working for you?

People are so interesting. We want everything quick. We want our apps to download less than twenty seconds, we want that app to find us a date, we want next day delivery, we want some kind of quick fastening device to replace our shoelaces, and you can apply for a loan in less ten seconds. But, if I told you that you have to make a change for your relationship, or your career, you would say, "Yeah, I'm working on that!"

Most of the attributes a leader possesses are for the benefit of others. A good leader will use them to benefit others. A bad leader will convince others that they possess these attributes, and then abuse the attributes and the people they convince. A poor leader is one who seeks to gain people and influence without first obtaining the attributes. In this book I call these leadership attributes *epaulettes*.

Leaders drive teams toward their vision, managers make the process work, mentors develop individuals, and coaches develop the team. You're in the race, but are you running in the right direction?

Find a way to celebrate your workers. It's not an empty message or the same thank you message. And, this will require some work to get the right narrative, but this is what relationship is about. Celebrating is a part of coaching. It's building people up. We build them up to set them up for the next step in thier career.

Training shouldn't be reserved for after someone makes a mistake. This happened often in the early part of my career. I once asked my supervisor to help stay ahead of issues with training. I was asked this question: what do you want to learn?

My response was: I don't know what I don't know. Can you just look at the workflow and worst card scenarios? When I received my first promotion in the Workforce Development industry, I trained on everything you can imagine. My team needed it too. Of course, some were too proud to admit they needed training and others swore they were good.

I had to find practical ways to connect with them and train them, but not cause offence. And then, I had to circle back to see how effective they were with the training. I also used a train the trainer model that allowed me to train on staff members and observe them training their peers. It's usually fun and it offers growth for the trainer, the team, and me. People took their training assignments seriously.

This is how politicians get elected to office. Their platforms appear bigger than our problems. And they appear bigger than their platform. As a leader you are bigger than the other. People must believe this and they need hope in this as they follow you – then they too will be bigger than the problem.

People report to their managers, but they will rally around their leader. We would be wise as leaders to rally our team around us and not the goal. We must appear to be bigger than the work.

Goal, prep expectation, mentoring, and or coaching after action review reward. Rinse and repeat.

It should be coaching and /or mentoring first. Address the worker or team disposition and then talk shop.

Look at some of the most successful leaders we have today. You may not agree with them. You may not even like them, but there is a draw. They bring out the ambivalence in us. We like them or we live to hate them. And because we misidentify love, or misappropriate the word, we don't leave them. They make us feel and that is what we want. We know we're alive when we feel.

Thinking is boring! That's right, I said it and you agree with it, but you won't admit this publicly. Therefore, some people stay in dysfunctional relationships. We want to leave but we want to stay. I went on a tangent there, but you get the point. Leaders make people feel. If you've been appealing to your team's sensibilities, you're boring. Your team is bored too. It's hard to motivate people who are bored if you're boring.

When you are your true self with people you cease to be boring. It's okay for leaders to make mistakes and it's okay to laugh at yourself.

Meetings

Gentle Reminder: Don't focus on a moment in time and forget the timeline.

You can micromanage from anywhere.

This is stifling and you may mistakenly think that this is keeping people in check. In fact, this is stifling to the team. This is only management on your part. You can lead from greater physical distances than you can manage from.

Don't manage employees with shortcomings. Instead lead them through the shortcoming. You don't want them to feel like they're just being managed during this difficult period. Of course, you'll have to lead yourself through your disappointment or even frustration, but you should not attempt correction until you have settled the situation for yourself. You expect a good outcome, you planned for this time, you sorted out how you feel, and you considered how the staff member feels because you had conversations.

This is where I went wrong. After discussing shortcomings two or three times, I would advise the staff member that the next step would be corrective action. When the shortcoming persisted, I would have it prepared and then call the person in to present the formalized document to them. I think it would have been more effective if I gave them the impression that they were helping me to craft the correction.

Instead of having it premade, I would meet with them and talk about how we could improve through this formal channel. I left them knowing that we will, together, put in place a plan that could help them. Now I already know the narrative the form for correction needs. But, I want to avoid being perfect and presumptuous to the staff member.

The one or two shortcomings are mentioned by me, and the option for a timeline to improve. This must be done delicately though. I don't need them to approve of the final version or, the action(s) to be taken in the event they cannot achieve the expectation. I would ask open-ended questions to solicit their input. I also want to tell them that we will meet again later in the week to sign off and acknowledge receipt of the correction action. I'm careful to say that their signature does not mean they agree. After all they can disagree, it's their choice.

I don't want to bam the person.

I don't want to scare or threaten the person into submission because the situation could then become a pseudo condition. I want to lead the person, to a better place. It's not likely that they can lead themselves or, they wouldn't have the issue right now.

I want them to understand that policy and production tolerances were put in place before them, not for them.

You need to be a coach here. You need a cache of success stories to share. There are many famous people who struggled with something and achieved in spite of it. I like to analyze what they dealt with, how they overcame it, and how their success helped others.

If you probe you get enough information to manage the situation and lead the person. If you pry you expose elements that you cannot effect change for and now you own it.

Managing stops or trails off at the conclusion of the shift, project, or contract. Leading changes the lives of others as it transcends the work. Simply put, if you're managing people, they'll get a check. Now, if you're leading people, they can not only get a pay check, but they can keep that job and grow on it.

You absolutely need to grow people as this will put them in the best possible position to handle adversity. I want to know why we're still upset about something that happened on Monday because today is Thursday.

That person we were upset with on Monday could have been wrong, but if it's Thursday, and I'm upset like it's still Monday, you know that's an area that I need to be coached in.

This is Beast Mode

Warning: Beast Mode should not be used by an inexperienced leader at any time. Results are not guaranteed and can vary by individual and circumstance. Reader discretion is advised.

This is the boss level of the video game.

When we met in the Intro, I told you I perceived, and I perceived correctly. I surveyed the landscape and I surveyed correctly. Here, in this place, there is much material without recognizable form, to the sightless. I lost the form of the life that I once had, but not my vision. What was lost is still here – it just needs to be reformed. In this place there is smoke – only this time I am the fire. This is *Beast Mode*.

People who run track know this: If someone is in front of you, protocol dictates that should one say, "Track," to alert the person in their path. It means move over. This will alert the person that someone is behind them and intends to pass. Yes, that's the tone I want to set in this chapter. Track means I'm not going around you or waiting for you, just move out of my way!

For a prisoner, this is vitally important as someone running from behind you can be a life-threatening situation. *Beast Mode* means, "I am determined, track, I am a force, and don't get in my way, track. You don't want to make me angry, track. I'll send the end that I expect because my vision of the outcome is clear." It's not a Jedi mind trick, it's not Sid Roth Supernatural, or a mantle that descends from the heavens, but you might think so.

If you're thinking you already subscribe to *Beast Mode* and apply it readily when needed and you didn't need my rendition of it, you're showing off – but I like that!

Beast Mode is attitude and its action, but it is not cursing at other drivers or inviting someone to fight – that's just anger. It's not repurposing bad feelings and channeling them into this new situation. It's not recklessness – it's unbridled ambition to accomplish a just end. It's for you. It's not for you to teach someone a lesson. This is about success, not revenge.

The average person will apply the right tools and strategy to a situation. The professional will consistently do the same, but *Beast Mode* is unadulterated focus, a penchant for justice, and "It's Monday, have my money." It's not that more is available to you currently, you just see it all, and you know how to use it.

You can build wealth and you can build relationships, but you can't build success – you take it.

You attain it by taking it.

Note: There are things we build and things we take. Wealth and relationships can be built, but success – we take! Winners don't make the trophy or fund the prize – they take it! So, why do so many people try to make success?

This simply cannot be done! Success is out there! But it's nothing you can create, you attain it, claim it, take it, track! This state of being is not done while we are being coached or mentored. You can't be coached to mentored into *Beast Mode*. It would be premature to think that because the opportunity presented itself, we must rise to the challenge.

Gentle Reminder: When opportunity comes, I want it to see me as opportunity!

I interviewed for a job once thinking I had a good strategy. The interviewer went on to share some important dates with me. Well, this was all I needed as I coached the emotions of the employer. I covered all that was appropriate, and then I found unique ways to bring up the important dates. I asked about the preparation, resources, and expectations for them. Soon, the interview shifted from me to the prospect of not meeting these dates. After I felt like my coaching was enough, I tried to mentor the interviewer by asking for a hiring decision in my favor. Well, you should know that I was rewarded with the job.

I get my stuff back.

Some years ago, I had to have my alternator replaced. After having it replaced, I believed the replacement was defective, but I bought it as is. I couldn't drive the vehicle back, so I had to take the bus. The conversation took place in the bay, but it was close to the manager's office. The mechanic said they would not replace the alternator, nor would they refund me my money. I said, "I want the manager!"

The technician said, "You don't want to bother the manager for this or anything else, believe me!" I insisted, and this is what happened. I was taken to see the manager who was seated eating his lunch. Only a third of his frame was visible when he was seated. He asked, "What is it you came in here for? Didn't the office guy tell you parts as is, no return, no refund?" I said, "First of all, wipe your mouth off when you talk to me!" And, "I gave your shop money to repair my vehicle just a day ago and today, I can't drive it. I don't care about your policy."

Now, when he stood up, it seemed like he wouldn't stop unfolding. When he did stop, standing with his back straight and arms extended, his knuckles rested on the table. This angered me because I felt he was using his size to intimidate me. He didn't go for my jugular – he went for my ego. Now, there's silence in the room. Now that I think about it, this reminds me of standing on the rubble of what I lost in 2019.

Well, on that day, I came to reclaim what was mine and I'm going to have it! The manager turned his head to the side and looked in that direction, as if there was someone else as tall as him in the room, at his eye level, and then he barked an order. "Give him what he wants!" It didn't seem as if the order was to a specific person, but people moved, and I was motioned to return to the bay area.

I got my money, and all ended well. The workers seemed amazed and I'm sure they thought I was crazy. What I think about looking back at that situation now is this: I was in beast mode, and I just watched the manager devolve out of beast mode. I think he was a tough guy and we all had the right to be afraid of him, but it seemed to me that he was relieved to exit his beast mode. It must be tiring to be that way all the time.

This state of mind or being should not be maintained over long periods of time. You're supposed to rise to the occasion, not live in the occasion. Watch this logic. Someone like him could not have yielded to a man bigger than he, as that would look like he was scared. In this instance, I was smaller, and so he got away with just doing the right thing which is a win for him too.

Beast Mode, Not Kitty Mode

My son remembers the most insignificant things I say. He will tell me that I said this or that and I don't even remember. He said, "You said whatever he was talking about."

I replied, "I'm the father, I don't have to remember what I said, you do!" Then I said, "You go now, and stop looking at me!" Can you believe he looked back at me while he was walking away? I know he's a young'n, but you don't look at people when you walk away.

Pass the Placebo

The official motto of the United States is *In God We Trust*. This is a profound declaration. It could have been, "In anyone that speaks nicely to us we trust." It could have been, "In anyone who says we can trust them, we trust." How very fitting, to place such a motto on currency. The very thing all Americans and use daily. It's the one thing that everyone in a nation perforated by state lines, will use.

There is *active* trust and *passive* trust.

Passive: If I give you a job, I trust that you will come back tomorrow. In other words, there's something in it for you.

Active: I loan you money and ask that you make an IOU for the money. There's something in it for me.

So, someone says, "trust me" and your mind wanders to think what's the worst that could happen and then your mind captures a clear picture of the worst that can happen, yes that that can happen!

It's like love. If we knew each other a short time and you tell me that you love me, you don't really love me. You might want to love me, and that's why you said it. You may want me to love you. You just hoped that I feel the same way or, hope that hearing you say this will make me feel the same way, but your agenda is, now you can justify anything that is introduced after this declaration.

Love is a feeling that comes from love the emotion.

I don't doubt that people feel love without the emotion of love. This version of love is anchored to the thing that someone declares they love. This source of love is an agenda. It's hollow, shallow, and, it will be conditional – consider yourself warned!

Now, someone can display or declare love, the emotion with the feelings that follow and it can surface just as the previous example, but emotional love is anchored to the person and manifests from there, from emotion. I know, what does this have to do with leadership? Love can cloud our judgment and it can undo the work of leadership.

It is often confused with lust. If you're a leader, someone's love can target you – look, we're human! Love is the most versatile emotion. It can drive us to save or kill, it can lead to charity or greed, and, love can get to your ego quicker than anything else. If you guard your ego you guard your leadership.

Garden Variety

It's like the person who needs your help. They come with a story, it has emotion, they're animated, and they tell you how much they need your help. Okay, I should get some space between their initial telling of the story and my process. If I don't do this, they will have successful raised my heart rate to match theirs.

We should be careful not to answer their closed ended questions in the affirmative as this can give them false hope, prime me to say yes, or delay them from finding someone else who is more suited to aid. With job seekers it's ones that are inappropriately dressed, come complaining about one of my colleagues, or tell me a sad story. None of this has to do with employment. I don't doubt that some of what they're going through could be someone else's fault, but it's their problem and how they present the problem to me will determine if or when I should engage with them.

Their words, emotion, questions, buddy language is all an attempt to influence you, to lead you to make a decision that is advantageous to them. Next is the promise. It as I call it, the promise particles. I promise, this is the last time, I'll pay you right back. Then there's the offer. I'll do this and that. It's manufactured sincerity, which is anchored to the situation not them. And so, when the situation is over, so too is the sincerity.

You'll need to get some space here because you weren't prepared for this, but they were. Before they reached out to you, they carefully planned their narrative.

Gentle Reminder: If you think you're The GOAT, you'll have to feed the goat!

You must feed the ego of the GOAT, you'll have to subjugate people, validate yourself, withhold information from people you think can threaten you, separate yourself, and at some point you have to declare you are the GOAT.

We can assume that because someone came to work that they are okay. We can even assume that because we asked them if they are okay and they responded, "Yes!" that they are okay. What's okay for this person? Do you really know? If your work force is the denominator, and the work is the numerator, then the greatest common factor, always present, is time, as it will affect both parts the same.

Save It

Remember when you were a child and your parents gave you a piggy bank? It was a novel idea as these money saving devices came in many forms and popular fashions. We were supposed to learn an important lesson about saving. Until we wanted the money inside of it, and then we broke into it.

The energy we used to break into the piggy bank didn't die. It was used to make purchases of something we desired like candies or some other treats. Then some of us grew up to use that same energy to break into grown up banks and take that money. I'm no bank robber so I don't know what they buy with their ill-gotten goods, but I imagine they buy things that this same energy would use to continue. If the energy we use is of a negative nature, then we should be able to predict the outcome.

Oil energy powers the world, but it doesn't have to. It's the energy in people behind the oil industry that power the world. You might think that so long as there is oil, the energy behind it will persist. True, but even without oil the energy behind oil will persist – it cannot become exhausted.

What makes energy so powerful is not in what it can produce over time, it's that it can be stored. Kept for a time of the wielders choosing. How do you measure power, by how much can be tapped, harnessed, discharged or stored? It's the latter because in this case, stored power energy is wealth.

It's not just that burning fossil fuels for energy creates pollutants. It's also the human energy behind the burning of fossil fuel energy that makes pollutants. Listen, the human energy behind save our planet resonates with solar energy which has no emissions. The energy behind it is clean.

If you're forty years old and ran at your top speed for forty minutes you would be tired and need rest for a long time, maybe even hospitalization. The point here is a period of rest and recuperation is needed. And, perhaps you should have metered out your running time. By comparison. Planet Earth is 4.5 billion years old and humans have lived on earth for a fraction of that time. Yet scientists believe that the known world oil reserves will become exhausted in just fifty years. We're running the planet into the ground.

But what if the energy a person or a team has is unproductive. How can a leader change this energy? People don't change. I think this is because the energy that drives them doesn't change. This can be translated into – you guessed it – storing some of this energy. I know, this doesn't sound appealing, but what if the person is looking to get something that will not be available to them for a week or a month? They'll have to wait, right?

What if the person sees that they were wrong but still feel anger or resentment? What if the person was right and wrong? Like they said the right thing to a colleague, but they said it in a harsh way? We can redirect this energy. Now, I won't proclaim to have a fail proof system, however, I want the person to see for themselves what this energy signature is doing to their career, their quality of life, and their colleagues – this is coaching.

I've had a few performance-based teams with some team members that quarreled for sales leads and credit for closing. I learned that just establishing hard and fast rules of engagement didn't fix every problem, as the nature of some of the team was more aggressive than others.

In most every case where I had an over performer, they were contented with telling me all about their exploits and how it drove them to success. It only took five to ten minutes of my time at most to take them offline to sit and talk. The added benefit was that it made me feel good to connect with them in this way. By taking them offline I could distract them, I could redirect them to focus on what worked.

I'll also call this an *After-Action Review*, which I would use for a poor performer as well. Now, this technique worked nicely when I explained to them why I was doing this with them. Remember, I caused them to see this shortcoming in the first place. I led them to check in for the *After-Action Review* to tell me all about it. Knowing that this is how we address this shortcoming made it more workable for both of us. In the case of the person that cannot get immediate gratification, I would ask, "What will you do now? How will you busy yourself until that day comes?"

Side Eye

Once I was eating some cake with coworkers and one of them pretended to grab my cake making me drop it to the floor. I was so mad because the cake was good. My coworker was sorry, but asked why I was upset because I still had a piece of cake left. It meant a lot to me because all the goodness was in the part that fell to the ground – I was saving that piece for last.

I admit I thought about that cake for a while that day, but I wasn't angry, just really annoyed. I still had to pick the piece up, wipe the floor, and think about what I had lost. I think it was that I also lost a feeling of satisfaction and pleasure. Yes, that is what the cake represented. Feelings cannot be so easily dispatched with. And, it seems that we sometimes like to wallow in this energy.

My son has a way of becoming angry when he doesn't get his way – this is age appropriate. Now that he's older I talk to him more and explain why things didn't pan out the way he saw them. I could often offer solutions that get him what he wants, and you know what, he will remain upset. I asked him, "Do you want to be upset?" He responded, "Yes!" You see, it's hard to downshift, even when you get what you want. He preferred to remain in the old state of mind, even when he no longer had to. He had a path to his land of milk and honey – only, he was taking bitterness to it.

Well, my kid was honest, but what about people who want to be angry and they don't tell you this? We may inadvertently cause people harm or discomfort, as my colleague did, and not realize this. It's inevitable if we lead people. At some point we're going to disappoint them. Please don't let your title or position get in the way of their feelings. If you become aware of such a situation, make every effort to talk feelings to their feelings. I mean, don't use logical examples to explain yourself. Talk from the heart. Feelings understand feelings.

Occasionally you may learn that a staff member resents another department. You can explain the logistics involved with that department, how they connect with your department, and all the difficulties they have – to no avail. I've had staff debate the merits of what others do to avoid ceding the point. It's not just that they don't want to be wrong with their assessment. They too wanted to keep their feelings.

Coaching for this person will have to be more granular. It's not just resentment. They need the *Epaulette's of Leadership*. They could stand to be humble and resilient, but the other epaulettes will support these two. This makes sense and is probably what some of their previous leaders has missed.

> **You can't just coach a part of the person – you're coaching the heart of the person.**

Make Up Your Mind Already

As I'm writing this book the sitting American President was fighting being impeached. I get it, it's the responsibility of the congress to address the issue, but support among politicians, and the public is split along bi-partisan lines. I get this too, but how did we expect a perfect person to rise to power from among an imperfect society? Elected officials, and especially the president, don't just represent the people in terms of their duties, but also to an extent, they literally represent the state of the people.

Our current state of political affairs is dysfunctional. Yet we tune in for exciting changes in hot topic issues and tune out when it's time to make a change. An outside observer may think that we like the dysfunction. In a way we do.

Remember when you were a kid and got a cut? You put a bandage on it and occasionally, you would poke at it – to feel a little pain. You know, they say you feel most alive when you're facing death. See there, feelings, emotions – that's what drives us!

A component of politics is intrigue, nuanced narratives, public outcries, mystery, and forbearing statesmanship. When we grew up, we had relationships that suffered, but we stayed past a reasonable time. I guess the excitement of what's next and the opportunity to complain about the same points of interest was irresistible.

I'm sure there were other reasons people overstayed, but leaving dysfunction is hard because were also leaving the feelings that we grew addicted to. Sure, we also stay because we want to make things right, but we will eventually adapt to the new norm. Like pain, dysfunction makes us feel alive. Our current president makes us feel something. Whether that is positive or negative depends on what party you subscribe to.

So, he might get impeached for breaking the law. Okay, but this was not the only reason. If we're honest, we'll admit that we supported it because we also don't like him. This is in large part based on what he has said or did. Impeaching him or the unlikely result of removing him from office will not change politics. To do this we would have to impeach our society. We elected the president simply by being who we are, long before the election.

Let me say for the record, and off the record, that we still must respect our leaders. Difficult as this may be for some of us. You see, it is impossible to degrade a person without degrading their office. *The Continuity of Leadership Chain,* along with every office and every person within it must be supported.

Respecting only those you like and disrespecting those you dislike means there's room for growth.

What makes us follow a leader? We might find things about them desirable to lead, their look, accomplishments, aptitude, experience, pedigree, and their vision. Reverend Dr. Martin Luther King referred to his vision as a dream. President Obama's vision was free medical care for all Americans. What they shared was that their visions weren't tribal. They were big, bigger than they were, and all the people stood to benefit from it.

People felt like they had a relationship with these men, and the visions of the future that they shared. I think people are more inclined to follow relationships than orders or instructions. And so, I think a party platform will work if you are already in an elected office. If you are running for an office, you need a unique vision – it's not a platform, it's a place in time that people want to escape the present to go to.

You're a champion of the people, not the cause.

Okay, I went long way around with this, but ultimately, we follow relationships that make us feel. You may even have to break with your tribal politics to meet the people. That's leadership – it's you. Leadership is a discipline for you.

King and Obama coached the emotions of the people with their speeches, which prepared them to be mentored into next steps and a call to action.

Leaders are not always popular, or right, for that matter. What happens when someone we follow falls out of favor with the masses? Have you seen someone continue to follow a leader that had a clear shortcoming? And, you wondered why they couldn't see how wrong the leader was? Well, the leader coached this person's emotions. And, now that they feel something, they don't want to lose that feeling. So, they're defending the leader, but it would be more accurate to say that they are defending the feelings that the leader evoked in them.

I once attended a martial arts promotion for a childhood friend. He performed all the movements the Sensei ordered him to complete and received a higher degree. I think he received a white stripe on his belt. To me, they were like the epaulettes that I speak of. Before his test for promotion, I saw all the students practicing their art. They carried a time-honored tradition with them. Not one of them smiled while executing their choreographed movements.

My friend took his test by himself, but he practiced with the other students first. At the conclusion of the day, the Sensei invited me to join his dojo. I told him I would think about it, but I was interested in Krav Maga, which means contact combat. I like it because of its practicality. After all, if it's good enough for the Israeli Defense Forces, it must be good enough for me!

The Sensei was appalled. He said this form of fighting was an upstart. He said it has no roots. He compared his form of martial arts to the major religions. He said he can trace his house of martial arts back thousands of years.

His comments didn't change my opinion, but it made me wonder about people who are leaders, people who practice leadership, yet have no formal training in leadership. I would not say they are not included in the *Continuity of Leadership Chain*, but without the structure and formal training, how can you effectively pass it to someone else? I mean, if you can't define it and prove or try it, how do you replicate it in someone else? I know it is possible, but important information and practices get lost if they are not established.

- How do you judge performance?
- Do you think the lack of staff and customer complaints is a positive indicator?
- How would you know how to support such leaders when they face unfamiliar challenges?
- How would you know at which point you needed to connect with them in order to effect the needed changes?

If this leader had been on a team, fraternity/sorority, military, or MBA program, then you know there was some formal training for leadership positions. Don't forget the initiations or hell weeks involved. This will weed out those who don't want it bad enough. No, I don't think having people do silly things makes them a leader. But after that, you know the person went through some things to get to the place where they can be taught, and most importantly in front of people who can, and want to, teach them.

Of course, there are other institutions outside of the ones I listed. I know some companies have academies, but tell me:

- How many of those academies are open to line staff?
- How does that training support quality of life for those who are being led, directly?
- Do you see tangible results in: morale, turnover rates, and production?
- Do you see quality candidates for newly created/vacated positions?
- How does this affect company online ratings?

Look, if you tried this approach it couldn't hurt, right?

It's weirder than finance how companies struggle to find candidates for vertical opportunities. Well, if you choose to subscribe to my version of *Applied Leadership*, where should you spend more of your resources? Should it be coaching or mentoring?

Leaders don't lead peace they lead pieces.

It's not a bad thing.

If you have direct reports and you expect peace, you're a manager. You're managing *Promise Particles*. You know, from the time the words, "I promise," comes out of someone's mouth you know that the things they speak of are not going to happen. They say, "I promise, you can trust me!"

Now, this writer has heard that many times. I have this rule of thumb. If you're trying to earn my trust, you're trying to set me up. Leaders draw this kind of attention for several reasons. Someone says trust me, and your mind wanders to think what's the worst that could happen, and then your mind captures a clear picture of the worst that can happen. Yes, that thing can happen! So, there are two entrances to the leader's ego.

Active is you leading to your ego.

Passive is other people leading you to your ego – the way the serpent did to Eve.

Take a look back at the intro.

Beast Mode is not reserved for training or practice. You're not looking for a coach or a mentor. This is a high profile, high stakes situation. I didn't say kitty mode, I said *Beast Mode*. All that you've been through and become has culminated into this moment. This is the cat's pajamas of performance.

Finish It

Off the Books

It's onus, not ownership!

Have you ever had a supervisor tell you to take ownership for some action or outcome? Well, that's an overstated word. When someone tells you to take ownership, it's usually not a good thing. Either something bad has happened, or something bad is likely going to happen.

It basically means we must assign blame. It's not a bad thing, but we need to know who will be held accountable.

That's another word – hold yourself accountable. The owner will feel slighted. They may find fault in others and they may be right to include others – case-by-case, right? This happens because they don't want to take ownership. Who wants to own something bad? This kind of ownership doesn't change hands easily.

If you know the exact date of your last employment, you're still upset about it. If you don't know the date of your last employment, you didn't learn from that experience. Thank you, for your silent honesty.

I'm not going to share my problems with my son nor will I complain about the solutions to my problems.

A friend of mine shared how he corrected his son's homework one day, and he made corrections in the homework book and wrote the word wrong on an answered question.

Now, his son's mother made a comment to the son, which the son shared with his father. The comment the mother made to the son was, "It's not right, he shouldn't do that to you." The son told his father that he explained to his mother that his father was only trying to help. The father, quite upset to learn this, told his son, "Your mother has a mouth and I have ears, she can tell me this herself!"

As someone who has worked in performance-based positions for over a decade, I know the importance of metrics, but I also know that numbers don't lead people. Teams can't rally around a number because they need a leader to do this. You don't want to push your team to a number as this would inevitably push them away from you too. You can't tell people you have a vision, scale it down to a number, and then tell them to go for it.

Recall when I shared the situation I had in the last video where I spoke about a negative comment someone made about one of my posts. I said leaders don't get into back and forth exchanges via email. We should talk to the person face-to-face if we can. Well, a similar situation occurred since then. But I failed to discern how similar it was at the time.

Below, is the actual transcript from my YouTube video:

Setup for Conflict/Step Up to Resolution

Every morning I ask my son if he's going to have a good day. His response is, "Yes daddy!" I then ask why. His response is, "because I want to have a good day!" At the tender age of seven he has accepted the fact that he leads his day.

This post was wildly popular. It received 164 likes, was retweeted 40 times, and received 10 comments. One person said at the rate my son is going, by the time he's of working age he would be the perfect employee, or something to that effect.

Her Response

So, what happens when he has a crappy day? Has he failed?

I didn't think this was an attack because she indicated that she liked the post with the little red heart. And so, I only wanted to provide clarity. I wrote:

No. This is not a test for him, and so he cannot fail. There is only expectation. He may not be able to lead all the events of the day, but he can lead how he reacts to them. I think engaging crappy situations with a positive attitude just might garner a positive outcome.

Her Response

You sound like a self-help book. I hope the child has someone else in his life to catch him when he falls. Never being able to grieve a failure is a very sad life.

Okay, let's analyze the comment. She said I sound like a self-help book.

1. Well, I wrote did write one and I believe in what I wrote.
2. There appears to be a fixation with failing or failure as she used both those words. That concern is irrelevant and misplaced. In fact, I addressed this by saying it's not pass or fail.
3. She went on to say that she hopes someone else is in my son's life to help him grieve a failure.

Now, let me ask you, what parent doesn't give their child positive motivation? And, for me to post these moments that I have with my son I must be happy and proud to have them. To say that someone else should be there for me is a slight. It was an attempt to throttle the exchange.

So there, I was baited. After her last response I did not respond. I know that I could not lead this person to resolution, but I can lead the situation – I walked away right there, a leader needs a measure of emotional intelligence to successfully resolve conflicts.

The key here is the leader's ability to understand their emotions and that of others. There is a sensitivity that is needed as well.

Know this:

Every exchange that is not profitable will cost you.

I want to add a layer to what I already shared. There are six basic emotions we experience.

They are:

- Anger
- Fear
- Surprise
- Disgust
- Happiness
- Sadness

And, there are six forms of energy. Emotions can vary energy. Technicians can measure our brain activity when we experience different emotions. They can see and record these responses with sensitive equipment. If you are happy, your brain will release hormones and chemicals into your blood stream.

Similarly, if you are sad you may be low on energy. Well, imagine an exchange where you are upset with someone. It will take some amount of energy to express it.

There have been reports of people who have experienced the emotion of fear. And they translated that electrical energy from their mind into mechanical energy that they channeled into their legs to propel them from that danger.

And some others have released their anger energy in a destructive manner – they went atomic. An example of that is road rage.

In my situation, the commenter's emotion and energy was of a destructive nature. Exchanging anger energy would not change hers to a productive energy, a positive outcome, nor would I profit.

Let's go back to childhood for a moment. Remember when we argued with another child for a turn with a toy? At first, we used facts to make our argument. You had a turn, now it's my turn. Remember the energy that was in play? But then, things spiraled out of control and someone said something about someone else's mother.

Former world heavy weight boxing champion, Iron Mike Tyson, famously said, "Everyone has a plan until they get punched in the face."

Let's analyze that. Our brains can generate electrical activity that we can identify as anger, which can be translated into mechanical energy of an arm moving, which can be translated into kinetic energy by virtue of its movement, and that can be translated into chemical energy at the site of impact on the subject's face in the form of bruising.

It's not worth it! I don't think diplomacy is not the opposite of a fight. No, it's the bookends to a fight. I would argue that it is better to end a conflict with diplomacy than defeat of your enemy, as they will return on another day.

Let's digress back to my situation with the commenter who resorted to insults rather than sticking to the issue which was in question – that was the bait to bring forth unproductive energy from me. What the commenter put on display were a complex set of emotions and energy that a rudimentary approach could not neatly address in a short span of time.

This is a case where I could not lead the person because the person would only allow their emotions to lead them, at least at that time. But, I can lead the situation. Why can't I leave this where we both believe we are right even if I think she is wrong? This leaves her intact, not attacked, and still having gotten her point across. You see there – diplomacy.

In this case there was no bargain to be had. Our emotional energy can get us into trouble, but our intelligence can get us out of it. I strongly urge you to look at Dr Ernest Jones' presentation on *Emotional Intelligence*. In his slide show, also called a deck, *Putting Emotional Intelligence to Work for Your Team*, Dr. Jones says, "An effective leader must be both aware and in control of the emotional health of the team."

How many people think that? I do! And I have shared this with my colleagues.

You're not only leading people but managing their emotions.

Kids sports leadership is emerging. Some are focused on the ballots, not about winning. It's about playing and having fun. Make someone team captain for the day. That should be a position, just like goalie. Develop a plan with this player. Have him or her direct some of the plays or practices.

If they're focused on motivation and cheering on their teammates, then they may have less time to focus on their own. This may help them to empathize with others.

Parents may not be equipped to deal with these kinds of shortcomings and hope their children grow out of it, but what if they don't? What if they never experience Emotional Intelligence or proper leadership training, and move into a leadership position?

I'm sure some children grow into this, but why take the chance? In less than ten years that child, a young man, will be behind the wheel of a car or dating someone's daughter.

My advice to parents is to study leadership, mentoring and coaching for yourself and for your child. I think it will add a great dynamic to your relationship.

If emotional intelligence and leadership were taught in schools maybe we would have less bullying, or maybe cases of bullying would be worked out without escalation. Maybe we'd have less school shootings.

There was one boy who got into a serious dispute with a player on the other team just about every game. Most of the parents and the coach would smile, commend him for his exuberance, and tell him to take it easy. But, I don't know if he ever was coached to temper his temper. At times, I had to restrain him from advancing on other players.

Earlier I wrote: Home is not where you live. It is a place where you keep your stuff. Home is in your mind. This is an important fact.

Unfortunately, there have been many rich and famous people with nice addresses that commit suicide. No matter how nicely appointed their property was or how many people would gladly trade places with them, they took their lives – that is a tragedy because there is no coming back.

I can't believe that all those people who have taken their lives wanted to go and never come back. Maybe some of them just couldn't see a way out of their problems. I won't say that my methods could save them. I only say this because it may be easier to change your address than a terminal mental state. So, home is in your mind, despite the popular saying, home is where the heart is.

People want a leader. If they need a fair distribution of resources, they want a humanitarian type. If they need to defend their interested from some sovereign state, they want someone bad to the bone on the battlefield. Yes, people want a leader.

Remember how God was leading the Israelites himself? And they were like no, we want a man to lead us, give us a king! Back in the day, a fictional cartoon terrorist organization, Cobra, wanted a new leader, and they created one. They took DNA from some of history's most notorious leaders, messed it up – I guess they added embryonic fluid and electrified it.

Bam! They got a new leader. Get this, even their commander who was their current leader wanted to create the new leader. And so, we want people who look like us to represent us, and tell us what to do if we like what they say. If they're tough, we're okay with that, because we associate toughness with strength.

I think people generally want their leader to possess qualities that they themselves lack. Or, we feel strongly about some issues, but we don't necessarily want to concern ourselves with the details surrounding those things. We like it when our leader talks about the issues and does something we don't want to do, and we want them to devote their lives to those issues.

We want our leaders to neatly and effectively take care of the burdensome work of sticking with issues until they are resolved.

Here's where we split into two camps. Some of us want our leaders to have a nemesis to compare themselves to, and others don't care for the bloody details. We just want to know what was averted and what was gained under their leadership. We elected them or supported them with the belief that they can fight through a fight if they had to.

Similarly, workers don't want their supervisors to complain about the company. Supervisor, you're a smarty – figure out a workaround. Coach me up to my professional capacity, mentor me to grow beyond that, and then repeat the process.

I strongly believe that if we can function at the higher end of our capabilities, we'll have less time and appetite to complain about the shortcomings that others have.

Frustrations set in when we believe that something beyond us is wrong and we stop doing what is right.

Continuing to do right in the face of wrong is leadership.

Remember, I said leadership is a discipline for the leader.

We're fickle too. Well elect someone to lead us, but leave them if they commit a crime. Then we'll elect them again in the future because we think everyone deserves a second chance.

I've seen some companies interchangeably use the words leader and manager. They ask, "What is your preferred leadership or management style?"

When customers are upset, they ask the worker for their manager. They never say, "Bring me to your leader," but when a company needs someone to turnaround a struggling team, they know this is an application for a leader.

Outro

It's your relationship to coach and mentor.

T he military places a premium on the importance of following orders. This is the hallmark of their *Continuity of Leadership Chain.* How do you get a similar buy-in from every person on your team who have no shared experience like basic training, or strict doctrine that must be followed? Well, if you're the leader.

Is your relationship scalable?

One of the criteria for a business proposal is that it should be scalable. This means you can grow it. Can you grow your relationship beyond infatuation, hard times, and expectations?

Open Concept Relationships are exactly what they sound like. For reference, you might see some people with an open concept floor plan in their home. This is where multiple rooms are essentially one as there are no walls separating them. Let's apply this term to relationships. When new, relationships seem like an open concept. There's opportunity to jointly explore this newly created space, but in the process of sharing and defining spaces, we find that we don't always see personal and shared spaces the same way. More importantly, available relationship space doesn't necessarily equate to an individual's capacity.

There are limits to our personal capacity, as it relates to relationships. These limits represent barriers or comfort zones. Barriers appear when one partner says, "I don't want to talk right now," and right now extends far into the future. Or, "I don't enjoy your favorite pastime as much as you do." And so, they withdraw into a personal space that is comfortable for them. These barriers can remain in place so long that that they seem impossible to remove.

It's where couples are actively looking for barriers in the relationship, and they try to jointly remove them that the open concept is restored.

Now, we've already established that these barriers are not physical – they're emotional or mental. There can more than one kind of barrier. Some can be fence-like, permanent, and well planned – there's a history behind building it. And they will tell you why they built it.

Others can be hastily strewn together, like obstacles which can prevent access and egress. This kind of barrier is employed for emotional reasons. Sometimes we don't know how to explain why we need this barrier – we just need it!

This does not include personal spaces because we all need some me time.

Let's look at this a little deeper. Personal space can take a toll on the relationship if it takes a substantial portion of the relationship space. Or, personal space can be relatively small, but if an unreasonable amount of time is spent there, it could make you a squatter in your own relationship. Take stock of the real estate you take up or refuse to take part in. You can't be with someone and happy by yourself at the same time. Don't let the elephant in the room be the only thing that displaces the emptiness in your relationship.

That's right! You make the first move, coach and mentor yourself, coach and mentor your significant other, make amends, make suggestions, leave your personal space. Why you? – Why not you?

You're the one reading a leadership and relationship book. Hey, it couldn't hurt. If you don't want to, you're in a relationship with your own ego. Take stock of the time and space you put into your relationships.

I'm Abrams – you're awesome.

Thank you for your time and attention. See you on the trail!

About the Author

Shawn Abrams has over 10 years experience in leadership. He has led military teams, corporate teams, and non profit teams to success. He currently works as a site manager for a community-based organization in New York City. He is also the host of the popular YouTube show *Leading in the First Person.*

Twitter: @abrams360media

FROM THE AUTHOR OF **THE SEVEN EPAULETTES OF LEADERSHIP**

T-MINUS EVERYTHING
~ AND COUNTING ~
THE LEADERSHIP & RELATIONSHIP BOOK

START YOUR COUNTDOWN TO BETTER RELATIONSHIPS
AND LEADERSHIP OUTCOMES

WRITTEN
BY **SHAWN ABRAMS**

EDITED BY GALADRIEL GRACE GRACE NOTES LLC IN ASSOCIATION WITH ABRAMS360MEDIA AND ABRAMSINDEX
FEATURING THINK LIKE A PROBLEM, ENDEAVOR, PREPARATION, QUALITY CONTROL, LOOK BOTH WAYS,
BY DESIGN OR BY DEFAULT, S,T,A,R, THIS IS BEAST MODE,TOO, CHECKMATE AND LIFT OFF

abrams 360 media   NEXT **5** MINUTES

www.ingramcontent.com/pod-product-compliance
Lightning Source LLC
Chambersburg PA
CBHW021405210526
45463CB00001B/233